Leslie,

Keep tell...!

Best,

For everyone who wants to tell authentic stories

and accept others' authentic stories

for better lives, connections and business all around.

Contents

What is authentic storytelling, and why should we do it?

From my days as a journalist, nonprofit executive and content marketing consultant in healthcare, it has been clear to me for years: People connect over true and authentic stories. But yet, it's harder than it should be for organizations to share their stories. We are stuck in the world of marketing to each other, though stories can actually set us apart more authentically.

This book will help you see the big picture of authentic storytelling, how you and your organization can get real and get started now.

Content marketing. Storytelling. Being authentic. Connecting with our audiences. These are some of the current marketing buzzwords. Let's not assume that they are bad. The concepts are great. It's the execution that sometimes isn't working.

They work, but they work best when they are not thought of as just marketing techniques. In fact, how about a little less marketing and selling to each other and a little bit more true connection through conversation and sharing?

Certainly, naysayers will scoff: Who has time to have a conversation with a brand? I don't even have time to have a conversation with my wife, let alone the brand that's trying to sell me hot dogs. Just sell me the hot dog. I'm hungry.

That's certainly a valid point. But I'm not just talking about brands that sell stuff we need, like food, furniture, etc. I'm talking about all of us – people and organizations. We all can, and do, connect around our stories.

Some people call it the Participation Age, where people participate and are more than a cog in the machine – as opposed to the Industrial Age, where they'd go to work and create a widget and were easily commoditized. Whoever demands the least amount of money gets the job. That worked because we were producing widgets. Certainly, widgets still need to be produced today, but you've probably heard that more and more machines are now handling those tasks. Or low-salaried employees.

Unfortunately, the Participation Age isn't here yet completely. I joke that there would be no rush hour – or rush **hours** in some cities – if we were truly in the Participation Age already. Rush hour is a sign of the Industrial Age. People go to work at a certain time, check in, have lunch at the right time, clock out and go home. Sounds like the Industrial Age to me!

Now, sharing our authentic stories – all of us – can actually help us advance in our careers, live better and more fulfilling lives and learn from each other. Anyone can tell authentic stories: People mostly! Organizations are people, too!

Authentic stories work best when they are part of the organization's or person's mindset. That's harder than "creating a piece of marketing." It's a habit. Authentic stories are not marketing messages. They are not created by a committee sitting around a table and saying, "Gee whiz, I wonder what our story should be." You know what your authentic story is by living it. If you don't like it, live (and then share) the next chapter differently. Authentic stories work best when people in the organization live the story. That story is then mirrored in the stories that are publicized through online and offline channels – like blogs, printed brochures, and social media – really any channel where you are communicating with people.

But what if the story that is lived by the staff or the story about the product is different from what's being shared in our marketing messages? Well, then that wouldn't be authentic. Some might even call it fabricated.

I've seen the best authentic storytelling initiatives take off when content marketers go to subject matter experts and ask them if they would consider publicizing their knowledge and stories.

The subject matter experts often hop right on board and are happy to do so. It's what they do anyway, and now they can spread the word about their subject to a wider audience.

The biggest hurdle often seems to be the extra workload and questions about how all of this content marketing and storytelling can get done. You could hire help, for example. But you also can do your own authentic storytelling without any help. We'll talk about how to make time a little later on. Getting help from a ghostwriter is also OK and does not hurt authenticity.

What about the people who don't want to? Or can't? Some people – mostly advertising people - are more interested in traditional forms of marketing. It would be easy for me to say they are wrong, that they should just get over it and hop on the latest trend. But content marketing has been around for over a hundred years, and people have been telling stories to each other, connecting around them forever. Around the campfire, at bedtime, on the cave walls. Storytelling is nothing new. We often just seem to lose the art of it all once we graduate from elementary school. Children are fantastic storytellers!

In true authentic storytelling, we live the story that we are sharing. We are what we are, and we care about what we care about. There's no work-life balance. There is work-life integration. And we don't even call going to the office "work." It's just another piece of our lives. I mention that here because some claim that our professional stories are different from our "personal" ones. Really, we are who we are.

We are living our story. We are part of it. So are the people around us. Not everyone will love us for it, but not everyone loves us anyway. Sometimes it's us who isn't in love with ourselves. There have been days when I didn't like the story I was currently living. You've probably had them, too.

What in the world am I doing here? Why am I associating with these people? And why am I working in an Industrial Age job when this is supposedly the Participation Age?

So when the story isn't happening the way we want it to or we are reacting to situations differently from how we'd prefer to be reacting, we can write the next chapter differently by living it differently.

It's easy to forget that we all hold the pen (or sit at the keyboard) of our own stories. While there certainly are many things that appear to be out of our control, there also are many things that are within our control. We always have a choice. Even when others try to tell us that we don't.

Sometimes we may have to risk a bit more than getting stuck in rush hour. But ultimately, our stories are up to us. We can choose to behave the way we are behaving, for example.

I encourage you to take charge of living and writing your story. That doesn't mean we don't need other people, their insights and support! We do. This book would have never been finished without other people's help. What kind of story would that be if there's just one person in it anyway? Ha.

Live your story, then write it – one chapter at a time.

How will you make your impact?

I was asked in 2014: "Where do you see yourself in 10 years?" I answered: "Wherever I can make the biggest impact on the most people sharing their authentic stories."

A couple of years ago, I did that at United Way where I helped nonprofits share their authentic stories. Currently, I do that mostly with hospitals around the globe, helping them learn how to spot, craft and then share their authentic stories.

Making an impact is important. How can we leave a lasting impression on our communities by using our skills for the greater good?

This book is another attempt at making an impact by doing something that I believe is important and can help all of us, not just financially but also on a relationship level.

Getting people to buy something once is not leaving a lasting impact. Teaching people how to move their marketing message from traditional channels where most people ignore them to social media channels also is not making a meaningful impact.

I want to make an impact by helping people and organizations be authentic with each other and build meaningful relationships through their stories.

Imagine if all our relationships were built only on transactions. You give me a dollar for that service, I give you a dollar for another service. But what kind of experience is that? Only transactional. It's a commodity. It's easy to cut a relationship held together only by a transaction. Plus, we go to the cheapest offering.

It's much harder to cut a relationship if it's formed around a shared story – a narrative that we believe in together. A story that connects us. It could even be a shared story of reaching a mutual goal. Shared experiences mean something.

I have a friend who once declined a job that appeared to be a fantastic career move because his current job – despite less pay – offered a shared story between him and his employer. They were connected beyond the money, though the money was good.

The same is true for customer-business relationships. It's easy to cut services that are a commodity. It's harder to cut services when we feel connected on a personal level.

Building meaningful relationships through our shared stories is a long-term strategy. I hope this book helps you and your organization, community and family get there.

Authentic isn't always perfect

Where do we start? Step 1 often is to admit that we aren't perfect. Nobody is, but of course we all want to look good and show our best (or better) side publicly. Why do you think makeup and Photoshop exist? Or why people get fired for saying something slightly off-message – even if it's true – on social media? Because we want to look our best. Why do you think people post mostly good things about themselves on social media? They are stories, but not often truly authentic ones. Sometimes they are an act. Sometimes, just the positive pieces of a larger story.

I think of most of my daughters' pictures that I've posted. It's always the ones where they smile and look so well-behaved. It's never the one a second earlier where they were grabbing the phone and arguing over who actually should take the photo. It's the good pieces of our stories.

But when we are authentic, we aren't always looking at our marketing-type selves. And that's OK. It's certainly OK to present ourselves in a professional manner. But lives aren't polished. And as more generations grow up in the digital world where many more things are public – sometimes including formerly private things – we will likely become more tolerant of true authenticity.

Maybe. My fingers are crossed.

I've noticed that my 7-year-old takes very authentic selfies and sometimes she even smiles. Will she fail to get a job 15 years from now because a recruiter sees her making a face in a selfie as a 7-year-old? Sounds silly! Especially when that same recruiter's Twitter photo looks no different.

People evolve. They are not perfect. I think more authentic photos make us appear more – you guessed it – authentic. And more human!

When people – and brands, too – are authentic, they attract the right friends and customers, the ones that actually want to be associated with them for the right reasons.

Instead of calling and interrupting everyone over the dinner hour, we live our lives and connect with those who are actually interested in connecting. Voluntarily. We don't mind getting interrupted by them. It's not even an interruption. It's just part of our lives. They are part of it.

Of course, we can still make the choice not to associate with certain people. That's fine. We don't all have to be friends. But we should respect each other's true, authentic selves.

If we don't understand someone, it's OK to ask questions. Many people have no problem sharing their stories. I've asked hundreds of people for their stories and hardly anyone says they don't want to share. Many have let me share their stories publicly. Others have done it themselves with my guidance.

Let's work on telling authentic stories and making meaningful connections. Ultimately, these habits bring business benefits, too.

Since I've started sharing my own authentic stories online, I've gotten all kinds of business from my blog in the form of speaking engagements, consulting gigs and other related projects. I have worked with many clients around the globe who have now done the same. It's possible, but you have to start.

Being 'perfect' can kill storytelling

Trying to be perfect has killed many authentic storytelling projects.

If every post on any of the blogs I've run over the years were perfect, each blog would – maybe – have one or two posts. Instead, thousands have been published. My Authentic Storytelling blog has about a quarter million (imperfect) words published as of 2015. That doesn't mean I don't aim for perfect, but at some point the publish button has to be pushed or the post won't get published. Our authentic stories wouldn't get shared without it.

Sounds so simple.

But blog posts, articles or anything we publish can be held up because we just have to read it one more time. Or add one more detail. Of course, at this point, we won't catch many mistakes, if there are any. We've read it 43 times already. And that additional detail? We don't really know what it should be, but we know there might be, probably would be, something, somewhere, that we could add. Sounds a bit wishy-washy to me, even fearful. Excuses are easy to find when we look for them. Just don't.

Maybe we have to run our article by 21 people for approval. Everyone fiddles with it. One person changes something. The next person changes it back. Once that process is complete – eight weeks later – the article is published. It's no surprise it didn't go viral in the first two minutes. Hardly anything goes viral anyway.

But it was perfect based on the time investment. Time invested does not equal value to audience. The quickest way to share authentic stories is to share stories that are near and dear to your heart. Things you care about!

Some things to consider as you are trying to figure out what topics might be best for you to share:

What do you catch yourself talking about (a lot)? If you have a lot of thoughts or opinions, this topic might be your passion and potentially could become a blog post. I say potentially because simply having opinions about one thing or another doesn't mean we should share them on a blog.

What's your expertise? What do you know a lot about? For example, I used to work as a journalist, and my career has focused on sharing meaningful stories. That's how my Authentic Storytelling blog and other sites started. Depending on the topic, it might be something worth blogging about. Unless it's confidential information for one reason or another, it's probably something that could become a blog. Or maybe pieces of it.

What do you do that you don't have to do? Something that is totally voluntary and that you enjoy. For example, I don't have to get up at 4 a.m. and go to the gym. I want to. I enjoy it. Since 2007, I've lost about 140 pounds, gained some back, lost some again, and am currently 100 pounds down from what I weighed in 2007. I even blog about this from time to time. The blog has garnered earned media by newspapers even, who reprinted blog posts and even did their own article on my journey to a healthier me.

Of course, if nobody else cares about our topics, what's the point? To get started, think about how people react when you talk about your passion topics. Are they interested? Or do they change the topic? Do they ask follow-up questions? These all are indicators of whether there is an audience for your topic. Or not.

But don't take these experiences in a vacuum. If you get a lot of offline non-interest, perhaps you just haven't found the interested audience yet.

You also could research what people are searching for online or what people are talking about on social networks – like Twitter. You can go to search.Twitter.com and search for keywords relevant to your blog and your experiences. It's so easy today to connect with others around a topic – even if we don't know each other, yet.

Or you could just start blogging and then find and connect to the audience as you build your blog. Sometimes we do overthink things! Don't create a process to manage the process of not getting something accomplished. I love the strategies where the strategy is to get it done!

It's not about being right or wrong

One of the problems with getting started with authentic storytelling is that many of us want to be right and be accepted when we share our stories. We can be so timid – almost like we are walking on eggshells – when we start sharing our authentic stories publicly. But people walking on eggshells will just break them no matter how carefully people step.

Before we even share our stories, we say things like:

- I don't know if this is the time to share this ...

- I think this story fits here. Maybe …
- You may find this interesting … (or maybe not)
- I don't want to brag …
- I wouldn't normally share this here, but…

We hand our audiences doubt. Well, if he doesn't think this is a good story, why would I? Don't place doubt in the listeners' minds before the story even starts. Just start!

Certainly, not everyone will find our stories interesting. Some people might even say that we are bragging when we share our successes. But successes should be shared! Brag away. Celebrate others for bragging, too.

We likely will never start sharing our stories if we continue to look for reasons not to share them. We should be looking for reasons *to* share them. Make them meaningful to others. Share something you've learned – without preaching! Share something fun and entertaining. Just start sharing. Don't overthink it. Don't get stuck in Approval Hell!

Some people might not enjoy or like a story. You can't win over everyone. But some people – let's call them your community or, if you wish, your target audience – will care, be educated and maybe even feel inspired.

It's OK. Seriously. It's OK. Not everyone will like everything we say. But those that matter the most to you will. To share your authentic stories, you have to tell them publicly. Don't apologize for sharing. Just do. Be yourself. Share what's important to you. Don't try to be right. Just be you.

The same is true with ideas. I've had ideas that could become a great product or service. You probably have, too. But just because we have an idea doesn't mean we can implement it. Though it can feel bad when somebody else implements "your" idea. If somebody implements my authentic storytelling ideas without me, good for them! And great for all of us really.

In general, when it comes to the Participation Age, sharing can help us all. And really, if somebody else can move our ideas forward, we should congratulate them. And ask for lessons learned. If we can do it ourselves, what's the hold up?

Just because I'm holding on to my ideas because I don't want somebody else to steal them, that doesn't mean somebody else won't have the exact same idea on their own anyway.

I talk freely about content marketing and authentic storytelling techniques, and here's why:

- It gives me the *chance* to be viewed as a thought leader.
- I can't possibly be hired by everyone who needs help with content marketing and storytelling. But being public does help me with work for hire!
- It's actually a form of content marketing. I'm proving the concept.
- It helps me connect with others who are interested in the things that are also of interest to me.
- Sharing ideas publicly actually helps articulate them and evolve them into meaningful projects.

I've talked about authentic storytelling in content marketing for years now and have trained hundreds of people who are interested in the concept. Many have stayed in touch and have taken on the art of authentic storytelling to share their business or personal stories. But there's still a lot of ground that can be covered for many of us out there.

There's still a lot of inauthentic storytelling going on. There are several ways for people and organizations to get started (all of them are OK):

- Read blogs that discuss the topic - like mine at AuthenticStorytelling.net and implement the strategies that are presented.
- Attend conferences and listen to expert sessions.
- Hire an expert to teach the in-house team.
- Hire an outside team to run the content marketing and storytelling project.

There are advantages to all of these options. Some people bounce back and forth between them. That's fine. The key is that as a community we'll get to the point where we share authentic stories with each other.

If you read my Authentic Storytelling blog regularly, it's no surprise to you that I freely share my stories and ideas there. Sometimes they are positive, sometimes not so much. If you implement any of my ideas, feel free to share your success stories.

Authentic storytelling is a mindset

Effective authentic storytelling, which includes social media participation, starts with the right mindset. Tools change. So do channels. Our attitudes can change, too, of course. But it all starts with our attitudes and mindset toward any given situation.

How we look at our social media channels is how we'll participate on them. If we think of them as traditional marketing channels – like billboards, TV commercials and newspaper ads – we will post things that are in line with those channels. That's when we end up posting crap like this:

"Our innovative product is now 12 percent off. Click here NOW to get this unbelievable deal. LINK. "

Does anyone click on these? Sure. The minority. Just enough people to make it feel like a success. Have I bought things off social media? Yes. There's a place and time to share some of your deals.

If we think of social media as a networking/getting acquainted tool, we will talk differently and will hardly ever actively sell on it. But that doesn't mean we don't make sales on social media.

A Trappe Digital client and I had this discussion:

"Think of it like you are at a dinner party. Would you even talk to somebody who is constantly selling his or her services?" I asked.

"Of course not. I'd tune them out."

"The same is true for social media. We tune out brands that only sell. We listen to the brands that offer interesting and compelling information. At some point we might buy from them if they are selling something."

"I follow that same concept offline," she replied. "I don't start a conversation by selling. I start it by connecting."

Social media is most powerful when we use it the way it's intended and in line with the way people use it: To connect with friends and others with similar interests and to share relevant, compelling information with each other.

Once we think of social media channels the right way, our social media participation will become more relevant for us and our followers and is more likely to pay off in the long run. The more meaningful connections we build online and offline also will help our stories. They become better and more people will care about them and even participate in them.

Storytelling is scalable

Is it easier for smaller or larger organizations to share their stories in a timely manner? Are authentic storytelling techniques scalable?

The answer is yes.

A single person can share stories – a lot of stories. The more people are added to the mix, the higher the number of stories can grow – in theory, at least. Larger organizations can share more stories because they have more people, and there's a higher likelihood all those people can add to the storytelling mix.

The sharing of stories, however, should not get harder or more complex. But it can get harder. I refer to this as Approval Hell, where many people have to approve every word of every story ever shared publicly. Unfortunately, those Approval Hell organizations are stuck in the Marketing Age, a close relative to the Industrial Age. Authentic stories don't need approval, though it's always good for somebody to proofread them for issues and mistakes.

Certainly, it can be easier for individuals and smaller organizations to get started, but the ability to share authentic stories doesn't diminish when the number of storytellers increases. What increases is the potential for unnecessary approval processes or mindsets not yet open to authentic storytelling across an organization.

Some questions to consider to enable authentic storytelling in an organization:

- Can employees share their stories publicly, or does somebody want to edit/censor them?
- Is the organization/leadership open to employees sharing their stories through blogs, social media, etc.?
- What's leadership's tolerance for what we would have called "negative" stories in the good old' days?
- Do employees know how to share their authentic stories in a meaningful way with others?
- Do employees want to share their stories?
- How will stories be shared internally and externally?

Depending on an organization's answers, storytelling becomes harder or easier (and in turn more likely). The easier we make it for people, the more likely they are to participate.

Storytelling is scalable. It already happens outside of organizations. Think about social media: Some stories are shared in smaller circles. Others get shared and distributed by larger circles. Some go "viral" – usually by mistake. There's no magic formula to make things go viral, or you'd see people do it all the time. I approve this book to go viral. Did it work? Ha!

People already blog about topics they care about. They talk about things offline, too. They share their thoughts and stories. How do we integrate what people do already in a company's mission in a non-forced, truly organic, meaningful way?

In February 2014, The Onion joked that "Online Content Creators Outnumber Consumers 2,000 to 1." The Ad Contrarian, a snarky and fun advertising commentary blog, reported that there are more English-language blogs than there are English-speaking readers. Competition for attention is fierce, I'd say.

And while The Onion thing is a joke, it is true that more and more people are sharing some kind of content. Not all of it is valuable, interesting or even consumed. Where organizations – big and small – can distinguish themselves is through unique, relevant, authentic content. That's why you need most everyone's buy-in and participation. It's the only way to get truly unique and highly relevant stories.

Organizational storytelling

Organizational storytelling happens when people associated with the organization recognize, call out, document and share authentic stories publicly. Stories help businesses (and communities) when they are true, meaningful and shared in a believable and meaningful way.

This is a different system from traditional messaging where marketing-related teams come up with organizational stories and massage the message. They then ask employees to share those messages. The ones that do are called brand ambassadors. Yikes.

Authentic storytelling focuses on spotting true, meaningful stories that relate to a brand's mission and are shared on a number of channels. We have to be willing to give up some control. Honestly, stories aren't very controllable anyway. But it can make us feel they are when we try to put approval processes around things.

In a true authentic storytelling setup, employees organization-wide share stories through agreed-upon channels to help the organization share stories authentically, consistently and constantly.

In a traditional command-and-control model, messages (not necessarily stories) would be written at one level and then sent to another level to be approved for the "appropriate messaging." This still works for many organizations, even today. Maybe too well, at times.

But as channels and technologies continue to evolve, this process will probably become more and more fluid.

In a true authentic storytelling setup:

- All employees are empowered to share their stories publicly.
- Storytelling is encouraged and explicitly endorsed by leadership.
- Employees want to share their organizational stories. They feel connected and can't wait to share their success stories.
- Sometimes people share stories that include things that can be improved. Nobody here is perfect. Learn from those stories and move forward. They shouldn't usually be fire-able offenses for the people who share them. Thank them instead.

We can't copy authentic stories from others

Let's talk about how it's pretty much impossible to copy our authentic stories. The decision to share our authentic stories is also a decision to be unique and original. We can't copy our authentic stories from others, because those aren't our stories, but are theirs.

You know how sometimes it can be easy to (over)analyze what our competitors are doing? They are on the latest, shiny social media network. So we join – even though we don't really know what to do on there. They use Tactic A, so we use Tactic A – or at least try to. When it doesn't work on Day 2 we call it a failure.

It's certainly good to know what social networks are taking off and fading away. It's also good to keep up on new techniques. But ultimately, the act of actually collecting and sharing our authentic stories is not that much affected by these things. If the Internet were to go away today, you could continue on paper.

In general, here's how you share your authentic stories – if you want to:

- Decide to share authentic stories.
- Collect the stories.
- Share the stories in a public and consumable way (those channels that offer a consumable way change from time to time).

This is pretty much how I shared stories as a newspaper reporter, later as a digital storyteller and now as I teach organizations around the globe to implement these strategies.

It certainly is easier said than done, but it's also not rocket science.

Knowledge of the latest tools and tactics is good, and I like to try new techniques and tactics to see if they help me reach the community members I want to connect with.

Ultimately, though, my authentic story won't change based on what everyone else is doing. That's my story, and I'm sticking to it. Ha.

Not all stories are positive

When all stories shared are positive, that's called marketing – not authentic storytelling.

And then you have the cases where we say a story is positive but it might not be. Once example of everything being positive happened on Facebook in 2014.

The network automatically assembled photo albums that highlighted each person's year. Users had the option of sharing the albums and could edit the default copy provided by Facebook, which read: "It's been a great year! Thanks for being a part of it."

This text, which was published by many Facebook users, wasn't always right, of course. Some years are great. Others, not so much. Most are probably somewhere in the middle.

I mentioned something along these lines on Twitter, and a couple of people called the discussion "trivial." Perhaps it was trivial because of when I tweeted it (during Christmas, when we want to enjoy each other's company), but the point isn't trivial at all.

Being authentic means that we call it what it is. If the year was great, we'll call it great. When it wasn't, we should call it whatever it was. In a perfect digital publishing world of authentic stories, we would also share our stories in a way that allows others to potentially take something from them or even learn from them.

Our lives don't have to be as perfect and happy as some of us try to make them appear on Facebook.

For the record, my year was pretty great. I started a new job at MedTouch, where I work with hospitals on digital strategy, formed Trappe Digital LLC and welcomed our second daughter. There are many other positives and also some negatives.

One of the photos chosen by Facebook for my year in review was my dark United Way office. I worked at the United Way agency in Cedar Rapids, Iowa, for almost three years. And while the move to MedTouch was great, leaving is always hard.

That photo being in there struck me as an interesting choice, but then I quickly moved on to the photo of my newborn daughter. Then on Dec. 27, I ran across a Tweet from Carlos Gil that said some Facebook users were reporting that the photos Facebook chose brought back bad memories. Exactly.

The Year in Review gathered your most-engaged-with posts from 2014 and compiled them into a chronological photo album, according to Mashable.

Clearly it's people's personal preference when (and if) they want to be reminded of negative life moments. I've had negative moments in my life that I basically never think about, and some of those happened years ago. When they do come to mind, I still feel sick to my stomach. Other negative life moments are only shared or re-shared publicly after some time has passed.

One of those moments for me was the 2006 premature death of my son, which I did end up writing about years later and which is included in this book. It took me eight years to push the publish button on that story, and it was the most read post on The Authentic Storytelling Project blog in 2014.

His death happened on Sept. 30, 2006, and I couldn't imagine being reminded of it in an album around Christmas 2006. I'm feeling a knot in my stomach just thinking about it.

I give Facebook credit for trying. Many people did share the albums, and I enjoyed looking through them. I did question the brevity of my wife's album, but in essence Facebook had the top highlights in there. One friend said she replaced some images. Not sure how I could have done that, but that's what her note said.

Obviously, I believe that it's great for all of us – the community and the person sharing – when we all share our stories with each other. But it has to be on the terms of the person whose story is being shared.

Good news is also worth sharing

Sometimes we may not share good news because we think it's bragging. We should share the stories that are happening in our lives. People – in general – enjoy seeing good news!

Here's an example from my local police department in Marion, Iowa.

In a Facebook post, police said they'd received a letter from a Marion father:

> *I want to acknowledge a great act of kindness and superior public service on the part of Officer Davis. My wife and I were traveling out of town on business, and my daughter was coming home from her part-time job at around midnight. She got a flat tire, the temperature was -2 degrees, and she had never changed a tire nor knew how to handle the situation.*
>
> *She was sitting on the side of the road, and Officer Davis asked her what the trouble was, and she told him she had a*

flat tire. Officer Davis changed her tire (in below zero weather) and instructed her how to change it should this ever happen again. He then followed her to put air in the spare tire and instructed her how to drive with the spare tire.

I want you to know how much this father appreciates public servants like Officer Davis. His exemplary service in helping out a young lady in need on a terribly cold night is a fine example of the quality of public service we get in Marion, Iowa. Please extend my deepest gratitude to Officer Davis and the Marion Police Department.

To which the police department added, "Great job Officer Davis!"

In just a few hours, the post was liked more than 800 times and shared 40-plus times on Facebook. People appreciate hearing good stories, too! It doesn't all have to be gloom and doom.

This person's comment summarized the reaction nicely:

It's nice to hear the positives instead of always reporting on the negative. There are so many more wonderful officers out there like him, and unfortunately we only hear about the questionable ones in the news.

This is a great reminder of the abundance of stories that are around us. Whether it's a positive law enforcement, healthcare or lawn care worker story, positive stories happen and are worth sharing. All the time. We just need to spot them and share them publicly. It's easy enough today with social media and blogs.

Marion Police could have easily filed that father's note away after sharing it with Officer Davis and maybe the chief. But instead, somebody took the opportunity to share it with a wider community by:

- Recognizing the story was worth sharing.
- Taking the initiative and sharing it publicly.

This is much easier said than done. Recognizing stories can be hard, and we can glance over them in our daily rush to get things done and checked off our lists. And even when stories are spotted, we might get lost in Approval Hell. Somebody somewhere might find a reason why something shouldn't be published. If we look for excuses, we'll find them! Somebody – one person perhaps – might have a negative comment to offer. Oh no. I'm glad they share the story.

And remember that 10 or 15 years ago, the only way for police departments (or practically any organization) to get stories like this shared would have been by pitching them to the local media. Some reporter may consider it or more likely would have said: "Oh, good story, but we don't cover things like this." And that would have been that. Who got arrested today?

Stories happened but were not told.

We all can learn from this and remember to share our stories – including positive (and negative) ones!

How public recognition shapes our stories

We also can share other people's stories. When we give credit where credit is due, that makes people feel good as well.

When others say out loud something good about us, it can validate our own stories and amplify them to others.

For example, I've known for some time that I work at a cool place at MedTouch. So I nominated the team to the Corridor Business Journal's Coolest Places competition. Once a nomination is received, the CBJ sends out an anonymous survey to employees to find out if the place really is cool.

They ask questions like whether your boss really cares about you and if work schedules are flexible, among others. A majority of local employees has to finish and return the survey before the business publication determines if a company is actually cool or just cool in that one nominator's mind.

It's a great process. In 2015, the MedTouch Iowa office was one of the honorees, and we even produced a video of the Top 10 Reasons Why We Are Cool. Very fun.

Public recognition means something. That's probably why people put so much weight into newspapers writing good articles about us. It's somebody else recognizing our wonderful story.

We can all help with this by recognizing and sharing other people's stories in addition to our own.

So recognition by others is important. And as I've said before, we don't become experts by calling ourselves experts. We are experts when others call us that. The same is true with awards like this. If it's just me saying how cool we are, it doesn't mean nearly as much as when others are saying it and when even more people see it and perhaps agree with it as well.

Public recognition is important. But before we get publicly recognized, we have to live it first.

Why do authentic stories need approval?

There is a tendency to have processes for everything. And there's often somebody who has to approve everything.

"May I say something?"

"Not approved." Ha.

That brings me to a question that often comes up: Do authentic stories need to go through an approval process?

In organizational storytelling, it probably will be many more years before the majority of stories can be published without any additional approval process. If ever.

But seriously: What's getting approved? The story's accuracy? Maybe, but that should be called fact-checking. What is really getting approved is whether a story represents the image we want the public to have of our organization.

That's good and bad, of course. Just because we want people to see us one way doesn't mean that this is how they see us. Lengthy (and sometimes unnecessary) approval processes can discourage employees from sharing stories that might be worth sharing. "Why would I go through all those politics?" an employee might think. "Is it worth it?" At least it's annoying and draining.

Most of this is really a holdover from marketing processes – when we only produced print brochures.

And people can just share their stories – including unapproved ones – anyway. Setting up a WordPress blog takes minutes. Setting up social media takes seconds, and chances are employees already are using at least one or more social networks anyway.

Then, of course, the question becomes if people want to live with the consequences from a story they've shared and that the powers-that-be didn't appreciate. And some authentic stories aren't appreciated by others in it. That happens because most authentic stories are told from our perspective, and, of course, all stories have more than one version when more than one person is involved.

And stories, even if not shared online, are very likely to be shared orally anyway. Those stories are passed on and passed on and passed on until they get back to the original storyteller, who can't even tell it was originally his or her story. You know what I mean!

The answer to authentic organizational storytelling is probably somewhere in the middle of all this. Let's dream for a second. What if…

- Leadership understands stories will spread – whether they like it or not.
- Leadership encourages open sharing and uses those stories to improve an organization's culture and processes and to celebrate successes. Let's not assume everything people share is negative! It's not. I have all kinds of good things to say about the day jobs I've held over the years – even during rough times, there were good stories.

What if ...

- Stories are used to celebrate employees.
- Employees share their stories with a purpose: What can sharing this accomplish (good and bad)?
- Organizations set up a digital playground where people can share stories. These could be successes, ideas for improvements and even current struggles.

Imagine a world where coworkers might read about a current struggle that they weren't aware of and offer ideas after seeing the story. Their tip helps solve the problem, and a story about struggles has been turned into a story of success and collaboration.

Remember to share with a purpose. No rants – at least not without an educational component allowed. "I hate Bob because he is so picky on what restaurant we go to while traveling" has no purpose. Asking a question or sharing thoughts on how difficult it can be to pick a restaurant while traveling with a group has the potential to be worth sharing. One makes enemies while the other can make friends because valuable information is shared.

Don't be upset when something does end up being shared publicly. It happens already anyway. We just don't see it because it's shared verbally.

It's important for an organization to publish stories for the world to see. Of course, depending on the business you are in, there might be varying degrees of proprietary information. We don't want to publish information deemed confidential. Depending on your business, there probably needs to be some review of content that might be confidential. But don't look for excuses, because you'll find them. Do an honest review with the goal of getting something shared.

But in some businesses, it makes absolutely no difference if the public were to know the details of some of the "internal" stories. This openness can help with recruiting and acquiring new customers and can even lift team morale.

Think of it this way: Somebody is featured in the newspaper or on TV in a positive way. This article will be passed around and talked about, and some businesses even laminate and mail it to people. The same could be true for companies and organizations as authentic storytelling initiatives ramp up and evolve.

Stories are the lifeblood of connecting, advancing our lives and feeling good about our communities.

It's not as bad – or as good – as we think

It's always good to remember that not all stories are exactly reality. They often are closer to the storyteller's perceived reality.

When I was on the University of Iowa football team in the 1990s, things were tough. Lots of losses, a transition from one coach to another and, of course, the media coverage wasn't too complimentary.

But I will never forget another player's feedback to a quarterback who was getting ripped in the media: "It's hardly ever as bad as it sounds."

And he added the flip side: "In the best of times, we probably aren't as great as we are made out to be, either."

I remember this almost 20 years later. When I have a bad day, it's probably not as bad as I perceive it to be.

My bad day might even be somebody else's version of a good day. #Perspective. When I have a great day, let's celebrate, but also keep in mind that not everyone might be seeing it that way. The key is to balance being satisfied and happy while staying hungry enough to go for another goal or improvement.

Our authentic stories are largely perception – by ourselves and by others. Which story is true? Unless somebody is intentionally lying, both probably are.

When and when not to share

Differing opinions of what should or shouldn't be published will likely never go away. In many cases, there might not be a right or wrong answer on what should and shouldn't be shared. By way of example …

A public safety official once asked for my opinion after he had shared a picture of a water main break – a public event. He had received some negative feedback. Below is a summary and analysis of the situation, followed by my recommendations.

What happened?

The public safety official shared news about the water main break on his Facebook page to provide information to the public and keep people informed. Another public official requested he not publish images or videos of similar events in the future.

Analysis

Several reasons are possible why somebody wouldn't want images or videos related to themselves or their organization posted:

Loss of control: It used to be much easier to control what was publicized and what wasn't – at least until the news media got involved. Being able to control what's published – as impossible as that is in today's world – can give people, especially if they are used to the old way of messaging, a sense of control.

The fear of looking bad: Not everything we do is positive, and even negative stories can help us build connections. Negative publicity isn't bad in itself, either. It's how we respond to it. Or how we shared the story to begin with before somebody else determined that it was negative.

Something else: There might be other reasons why this person wouldn't want content to be published. Ask them. The only dumb questions are the ones that we declare to be dumb: "This is a dumb question, but..."

Recommendation

In general, I believe the sharing of informational and/or educational information is very valuable to an organization. It builds trust with audiences, which, in this case, includes a city's residents. When information is shared, people can be informed and in the know.

At times, we have to weigh how the publishing of information will affect offline relationships. For example, is it worth damaging a relationship over the publication of public images or video? Your audience might think it is – since the image helped them know what was going on. You may or may not agree. Publish the stories you deem worthy of publishing. Just be aware of potential consequences and your willingness to live with them.

As a final note, a photo or video of a water main break hardly reflects negatively on anyone. Water main breaks happen. They get fixed. I did not see any negative outcry in this case from the public. We certainly can overthink things.

Where ideas for stories worth sharing come from

Stories happen all around us. Constantly. I bet we miss more than we notice. Some are super routine and nobody wants to consume them anyway. Others are just overlooked. As long as we continue to go story shopping as we move through our daily lives, we should be able to catch many stories worth sharing and consuming.

Story shopping refers to keeping an eye out for stories in our lives and inside our organizations that might be worth sharing.

Think of it like window shopping. We look, see things, evaluate what we like and then buy. Story shopping is the same. There are many stories happening around us. All are worth something. But some are worth more to some audiences because of their relevancy or because they solve that audience's problems.

Story shopping is important because organizations and people can't possibly share **all** stories that are happening around them. We have to be somewhat selective. So we shop and share the best stories.

When I share stories on Twitter, sometimes people want to know more than I can share in a Tweet:

- What prompted it?
- Who **exactly** was involved?
- Tell us more! Tell us more! Tell us more!

Usually, that's the case when people think there's something else behind the story, something juicier than what's already being shared.

Certainly all Tweets and blog posts are triggered by something. It doesn't always have to be something happening in our offline lives. Sometimes nobody else is involved. It can be another Tweet that got us thinking. Our brains might wander for a few hours and we form our own opinion on the topic and send out a related (but not necessarily similar) Tweet to the one that started it hours earlier. We may share our own story and pieces of a personal experience that ultimately were triggered by something we read earlier.

Sometimes blog posts are triggered by a combination of things:

- A blog post we read
- A headline we saw in an e-newsletter
- An offline comment by somebody at the water cooler

All items are totally unrelated, but they end up getting us thinking about one topic that leads to one specific post. It happens. And it's OK. It doesn't necessarily mean that the writer is trying to show somebody off, is venting inappropriately (whatever that means) or is doing anything else other than sharing thoughts and stories.

Sharing thoughts can be a great way for people to reveal their authentic selves. These might not always be their authentic stories – as in "here's what has happened" – but they certainly reveal people's thoughts, opinions and sometimes even their thought leadership ideas. Some of these thoughts are worth reading. Some are still in the evolution stage, which is fine, too, and a great way for people to grow. Authentic storytelling helps with that, too.

Ultimately, it might not really matter that much what prompted us to share an interesting or thought-provoking blog post. What counts is that it's thought-provoking and interesting and at least an authentic thought.

But, why might it be important for readers to know where a story originated? There are several reasons:

- There might be an even better story there.
- Knowing a story's origin allows us to decide whether or not we believe it.
- We simply want to know.

But sometimes there's nothing else to a story than what already has been shared.

Listening is key to authentic storytelling

One of the best content gathering/interviewing/brand journalism techniques is to simply listen to people. Listening unveils the best authentic stories.

But listening can be hard. It's our turn to ask a question or to share a tidbit. Why should we give up our turn to speak? Because we love stories! Other people's stories especially.

And the only way to hear other people's stories – including their version of our stories – is to give them time to share while actually listening!

Listening to others involves a number of skills that make the process easier.

First, be approachable. I've had people come up to me and just start sharing. "You won't believe what just happened!" Don't interrupt and start guessing what may have just happened. Let them tell the story. They will stop when it's done. Usually, stories shared are stories that make us feel happy or stories that make us mad. Stories that evoke emotion are shared. Routine stories are often overlooked –for good reason. Who wants to hear about the uneventful commute to the office? It happens daily!

Shhhh. Don't think it's your turn to talk when you've come to a quiet moment in a conversation. It might feel like it's your turn to talk. And it might be, but let the silence go on for a bit. Give the other person time to breathe, and they most likely will want to fill the silence. That will lead to them to continue to share their story, or a new one.

Ask good follow-up questions. Don't just go into interview mode and ask the questions on your list. Ask questions that you'd ask if this was a conversation – which good interviews always are. When somebody says, for example, that they traveled to 23 countries before age 15, ask how that happened and what the countries were. "Tell me more" is also a good follow-up statement that elicits more information.

Watch body language. Body language can easily be misinterpreted. You don't want to overanalyze it, but it's good to watch for clues about what a person is thinking or perhaps not saying. Bottom line: Don't guess what a particular body movement means and share it when you write a story. Use the observation to think about what to ask next during the conversation.

More interviewing tips

After two decades of authentic storytelling, I can assure you that most people want to share their stories. People want to talk, connect and share experiences. It's what we do.

But it can feel different when the person sharing the story knows his or her story will be publicized. Why?

- People want to look good.
- People want to sound smart.
- People want the story to be accurate, but accuracy can be in the beholder's eye. The interviewer's impression of a story – especially when witnessed first-hand – might be different from that of the person telling the story.

Of course, there are ways to make this process more comfortable for the person being interviewed:

- Listen closely.
- Display open body language. Show that you care and are interested in the story.
- Ask clarifying questions: "Did I understand this correctly? Is this what happened?"
- Let the person know he or she can see a draft of the story before it's published. This was a big no-no when I worked as a journalist in the early 2000s, but I used this technique in the days of Eastern Iowa News, a local community news startup I founded in 2009. At Eastern Iowa News, the practice helped with accuracy and sometimes caused people to think of another fact that was worth adding. Sharing stories before publication is the norm in organizational storytelling. That's not a necessarily bad thing – unless we get hung up in Approval Hell.

Listening closely and building a meaningful connection with the subject of a story can help us build stronger, more authentic connections and, in turn, help us share better, more accurate and more meaningful stories.

How to get started sharing authentic stories

Getting going

Ultimately, authentic storytelling – whether on behalf of a business or ourselves – should be about the sharing of information that is relevant to a group of people. That group of people can be small or large. Audiences for some topics are rather small, but if they are passionate about the topic, that's still a viable audience.

Most authentic storytelling strategies take at least a year to develop and start to work.

You need to get buy-in from others. Whether it's a personal brand or for an organization, others are impacted. My family has to buy in to a degree that I spend time blogging. It can take away from time with them – even if I'm blogging right next to them. If we are leading an authentic storytelling project for our business, somebody needs to do the work and get paid for it. We need executive buy-in.

The key to getting buy-in and keeping it:

- **Executive buy-in and expectations**: Make sure decision-makers understand the timeline. Think of it this way: Most executives didn't become executives overnight. It took time and lots of work to get there.
- **Team buy-in:** Make sure to celebrate the small successes and enjoy the moving-forward part. Authentic storytelling pays off long-term. Did I mention that it takes time?

- **Relevant content:** The best intentions will fail if content is not relevant to audiences, doesn't solve an audience's problem or is written in marketing speak. Unlearning marketing speak is actually a very hard task. That's why I believe (based on my own experiences) that journalists make great authentic storytellers. They were not trained to write in this overpromising, buzzword-rich marketing language. Once you've learned how to write in marketing speak, breaking the habit is like unlearning a language in which you are fluent.
- **Constant:** Content needs to be shared constantly. Twitter streams, for example, move quickly and for some users can turn over completely in seconds. Our attention spans are short, and our time is limited. We consume what's there and what's relevant to us. We have to earn and re-earn audiences' attention over and over and over.
- **Consistent:** Don't constantly change what you talk about. Pick a topic, define it and talk about that. You can't be an expert in everything.
- **New things:** Share what's new. People pay attention to new stories. There's a huge difference between just coming up with an outrageous (and new) opinion and sharing actual new things of value. Try to offer something that is new, interesting and authentic.
- **Just go:** Sometimes it's just best to not ask for permission and just go. Publish relevant content and show that it's working. Sometimes that can mean that

content is produced in weird places – like on planes or waiting for meetings – and on non-traditional devices like the iPhone, for example.

I like to use this exchange to demonstrate what happens when we ask for permission:

"May I challenge the status quo?"

"No."

If we are unsure, it's easier to shut down the idea. Permission is really only useful for one purpose anyway: When it doesn't work, we can blame it on the person who gave us permission. Let's own it!

Sometimes we can't ask for permission. We just have to do what's right, and people will see that it was the right decision. Sometimes it's an educated gamble. And sometimes the right decision might look like the wrong decision. Things happen. Learn from it and do it better the next time.

Sometimes, if we ask, we won't do it. We might not get an answer or permission. We overanalyze. We weigh the perceived and real risks – mostly perceived.

We don't know for sure if something is going to work. Things are fine. We don't need to push the envelope. We are comfortable in the box and prefer to only think outside of it but not *do* anything outside of it.

When it comes to authentic storytelling and content marketing, some people still think of the two as traditional marketing where we try to control the uncontrollable message. In traditional marketing, we message to each other and find the exact phrasing that will make somebody buy from us.

Good luck. That perfect phrasing hardly ever exists. Most of us cannot create it. But all of us can be authentic and share our educational and inspiring stories with each other.

Authentic storytelling is about being authentic, transparent and relevant. And yes, people can buy from you and me.

So how do we weigh the potential downsides to not asking for permission? We have a choice. If it doesn't work, are we willing to live with the consequences? Does the potential success outweigh the potential failure? Would it be worth it? If the answer is yes, consider it. If no, don't. It sounds so simple. I'm gambling that this whole authentic storytelling thing works and people care about it. So far, I think I'm on a winning path and many are coming along!

Now, not asking permission doesn't mean breaking the law or deliberately hurting people. Don't do that!

It means that sometimes we take a risk when it comes to sharing our authentic stories and helping others share theirs. Are we willing to take the risk, and it is worth it? Sometimes it is and sometimes it's not.

Asking for permission is really only important so we can blame somebody else when it didn't work anyway.

Another thing that keeps us from sharing authentic stories is the trap of perfectionism. Striving to be perfect is a good goal, but don't let it stop progress. Define your topic of expertise, decide what there is to talk about, talk about that and publish, publish, publish. And, of course, remember to promote your content. Don't count on "build it and they will come." Set the expectation early on that not all stories are perfect. Even though it's OK to strive for perfectionism.

In addition to these initial steps, there are a few more things to consider to get started.

Three distinct steps:

- Deciding what topics we want to talk about and deciding to get started.
- Agreeing on workflow – who is doing what, when and how long will it take – even if it's an estimate!
- Maneuvering office politics is something not to forget about!

The last point, depending on our workplace, can sometimes be the hardest. Changing how stories are shared from the traditional marketing model can be scary, and it's likely somebody will fight it. This can happen openly or covertly.

Sharing authentic stories takes a bit of conviction, guts and motivation. The more difficult it is to maneuver the office politics working against such storytelling, the more likely it is the effort will fail.

These steps can help you find your way through office politics and get your authentic storytelling strategy off to a good start:

- **Identify your advocates on all levels**. Who is on board and who isn't? Who is willing to voice their support and help influence others? Remember that advocates on all levels of an organization can have influence. Sometimes a rank-and-file employee will have influence far beyond his or her job title. Identify those internal leaders and educate them about authentic storytelling. Ask for their support.

- **Identify influencers of internal leaders.** Leaders in many organizations are influenced by people from the outside. In a nonprofit, the CEO is likely to listen to his or her volunteers. Friends of a leader in your organization might use your product. External feedback to internal leaders, when it's positive, moves projects forward.
- **Check in with your executive sponsor or main advocates.** Make sure your main advocates are up to speed on how things are going. That way, they can share successes and continue to advocate for the project with others.
- **Share successes as publicly as possible.** The more people who know, the better. Definitely share stories with leaders. If possible, share some successes on a blog and – depending on your market – share them with the media or a local, regional or national journal that covers your industry. Successes are celebrated. Remember the time when people announced they just launched responsive websites? That used to be news because it was a new thing. Kind of crazy when I think of that being news today.

Sharing authentic stories shouldn't be that difficult: identify the story, document it, publish it. Grow as a business because people who believe in your stories join you as customers.

But just like office politics can eat company strategy for breakfast, it can eat authentic storytelling for lunch – especially when we aren't watching what the current perception is of the authentic storytelling initiative.

Many projects can be and are influenced by office politics. Instead of complaining about how nice it would be if there were no office politics, we might as well acknowledge them and figure out how to maneuver through them. Complaining only hasn't changed anything, yet.

The better we are at identifying office politics in our authentic storytelling plan and figuring out how to manage them, the more likely we are to get the program off to a great start and a successful on-going implementation.

Yes, the time spent maneuvering office politics and outdated processes is inefficient. But if we don't acknowledge the politics, they can stop good stories from being shared publicly. And you know what happens to stories that aren't shared: They die – for the most part. Until somebody else – like the newspaper – decides to share them for us. And they might have a different perspective on them.

The so-called 'organizational opinion'

Sometimes businesses get hung up in the "organizational opinion," which also can slow down storytelling.

You've probably heard it:

- What's the organization's stand on this?
- What does the organization say about this?

- So and so is (or isn't) representing the organization's opinion.

And I wonder: Can an organization have an opinion? Of course not. But the people who are part of an organization – collectively or individually – can. The opinion is either the opinion of a decision-maker or a group of them. Many times it's not even an opinion. Organizational opinions sometimes are closer to safe answers, such as "We support the best." Sometimes they are so-called compromises between a leadership group. They couldn't agree on an opinion.

Sometimes organizational opinions sound like this:

- We don't comment on this kind of thing.
- We have to evaluate all of the facts before saying anything else. Good luck with that one. **All** the facts. Ha.
- We agree with whatever so-and-so agrees with.

Doesn't "we don't have an opinion" actually mean "we do have an opinion, but we don't want to tell you"?

Everyone has an opinion. Even journalists have opinions, despite trying so hard not to have them.

Opinions sometimes aren't safe and not everyone will like them. And organizational collectives can have one opinion, and individuals who are part of that collective can have another opinion.

Ultimately, it comes down to this: What does an organization stand for, and what do its members believe in and try to accomplish? It's really very similar to personal brands. It does get complicated when people inside the organization aren't aligned.

The organizations that have defined this well will likely never have to give their "organizational opinion" for specific events ever. People know what it is, even without somebody massaging the wording for a specific response. The opinion doesn't change from day to day. It is what it is. And the people who are part of the organization will support the collective opinion because it's what they live and believe. Authentic living and storytelling at its finest, really.

It's OK to have opinions – especially when they are authentic and have been defined by what we do every day and aren't decided for specific events happening right now.

With organizational opinions come "internal" and "external" stories. Usually when there's a need for two versions, the internal story isn't all that positive. Or the organization is still messaging and not yet truly participating in authentic storytelling. In a true authentic culture, alignment is a moot point. It's all the same story.

When it comes to story alignment, a few questions come to mind:

- Why is there an internal story AND an external one?
- Which one is more accurate? Probably the internal one.
- If the external one is more positive than it should be, isn't it actually messaging?
- Can anyone share the external story with a straight face? People probably can share the accurate, internal

one. Of course, the perception of accuracy can depend on the individual.

- Can anyone actually keep track of which story is supposed to be external and which one isn't
- If the stories don't align, do we just share no story at all? Probably. People don't want to live with the consequences!

Story alignment in authentic storytelling isn't about messaging a perfectly spun story. It's about deciding what your actual story is, then sharing it. If you don't like the actual story, the most authentic thing to do is:

- Determine why not.
- Change our actual story – explain honestly what we are doing.
- Share the new story.

But it's so much easier to come up with a message. "This sounds good. So that should be our story."

Inauthentic stories can work in the short term. They even can help lead to short-term financial success. But what if they are found out? Relationships can suffer and long-term success might not happen.

In addition, it's almost impossible for people to share inauthentic, untrue – even partially untrue – stories with their networks long-term.

So why not determine what we stand for, live our story and tell it authentically? It sounds easier.

Part of it comes back to the notion that messages can be controlled. Sometimes they can be or at least they can be shaped. For the most part, stories can only be controlled by the way we live them. Live them the way you want them to be told.

Coming up with your value proposition

It's still important to define your value proposition to your audience. Why should they care about you and the things you talk about? What do you have to say that is important? Defining your value proposition also can help staff be on the same page and help your business be even more customer-focused. After all, you have to have customers to be a business. A business without customers is a hobby.

What's a value proposition? A value proposition specifies the value your business brings to the customer. Value focuses on the customer – the person who consumes your product. It doesn't focus on why the business owner has a business (a passion, for example). Passion certainly could be part of the business' story but not necessarily its customer-focused value proposition.

Here are some examples that explain how to verbalize an organization's value proposition.

Steps to your value proposition

In 2009, I launched Eastern Iowa News, a community-based news start-up. Initially, I wanted to learn about publishing through WordPress and running a website. I had some experience with an older, non-WordPress version at The Gazette in Cedar Rapids, Iowa, and in the 1990s, I had a Geocities site, a service later bought by Yahoo and then shut down in the United States.

I'd also continued to run across community-newsworthy items on my commute and while out in the community. I wanted to share those items and learn about WordPress publishing.

That's a good personal reason for launching the project, but it probably doesn't sound all that interesting to potential consumers.

Identify your customers

In the case of Eastern Iowa News, who was the customer? I identified the customer as the visitors who stopped by to consume content, the site's advertisers and also the contributors. In general, none of the contributors received pay for their submissions, so it's probably fair to call them customers, too.

Identify why they are your customers

Visitors stopped by my website for interesting content that they hadn't seen elsewhere. Contributors submitted content because they had something worthwhile to share, and they had nowhere else to share it where a large, relevant audience would see it. Advertisers bought ads – sometimes contextual – because a relevant audience had started to build. (120,000 visitors in Year 1.)

Summarize reasons (a.k.a. the value proposition)

Try to summarize the reasons, in a sentence or two, why you have the customers you do.

OPTION 1

Eastern Iowa News offers a moderated place where community members and journalists share relevant, community-level news that is available nowhere else and is of interest to people in Eastern Iowa.

OPTION 2

Eastern Iowa News is an online news resource for the region that does what printed weekly newspapers have done for decades: Report neighborhood news. Except we do it in real time.

You can find a number of templates for writing a value proposition online as well. There are many good ideas, and one may work better for your business than another.

I also like the template suggested by The Methodologist site: "We help X do Y doing Z." In the case of Eastern Iowa News, the value proposition could become:

OPTION 3

We help community members and people with information connect in one place. It's kind of like Facebook except that we check content before it's published and add additional contextual and relevant information.

Even businesses that haven't spelled out their value proposition probably have an implied value proposition. Spelling it out can help staff and consumers understand what a business does and what makes it special.

Depending on how short your value proposition is, it could end up being used in promotional materials and even turned into a tagline. If people would wear the tagline on a t-shirt, you are onto something.

Remember though: The value proposition still needs to be authentic and truthful. It's not a marketing message. It's there to help us focus on, clearly define and remind us what our value is to our interested communities.

Our value proposition is never: Because we want to make money. That's an outcome.

Defining your brand's voice

As more and more personal and organizational brands tweet, Facebook, blog and publish their stories and content on old and new channels, it's also important that you think about your brand's voice. Your brand voice is how you sound when you write Tweets, respond to Facebook questions, respond to emails and write your blog posts.

Now, we don't have to overthink this, and in true authentic storytelling, our voice is what it already is. But it's good to put some thought behind this, especially for organizations.

What should your voice be?

Your voice should reflect your style and way of doing business. It's similar for personal and organizational brands.

If you have a fun, quirky coffee shop that caters to new technology lovers, your brand's voice should fit that audience. Perhaps you could define it as: Fun, quirky, on the cutting edge, but not offensive.

If you are a serious attorney's office, your brand voice should reflect that. It might be defined like this: Serious, informational, trustworthy, but not chatty.

I like to use two to three words that describe a brand (Do this) and another set of cautionary words (Do not do this). It helps people communicating publicly for a brand (especially when there is more than one person) to have a bit of guidance.

For my own personal brand, I share most of what I have to say on Twitter, Facebook, LinkedIn, Instagram and my blog at AuthenticStorytelling.net.

I don't wear my beliefs on my sleeve. I put them on Twitter. Ha. That's true for the topics that I focus my authentic storytelling around:

- Storytelling
- Communication
- Leadership
- Technology
- Content marketing
- Social media
- Fitness (to a lesser degree)

I never actually sat down and wrote a formal plan on what my voice would be. It has definitely evolved from just chit-chatting to a more focused discussion. I would describe my own voice now as: Sharing, personal, chatty (sometimes snarky) and responsive, but not over-promotional (or serious).

Defining your voice

These questions might help you define your voice:

1) How would you describe your typical customer?
2) How would you describe a customer group that you would like to engage with but haven't yet been able?
3) How would you talk to them?
4) How would you describe the atmosphere in your business environment? This could be in your store, over the phone, etc.
5) How do people talk to each other there?
6) How would you like your business to be described by the public?

The answers could give you a clue as to what your brand voice might be.

Let's take a hypothetical company that would answer our questions this way:

1) Older, established business people. Connected.
2) Younger business people who are up and coming. We think they know of us, but they aren't extremely loyal yet.
3) Friendly, informational, educational, not too stiff.

4) Friendly. Business-like. Helpful. Cordial.

5) Like they enjoy being there and catch up.

6) Helpful. Easy to work with.

Potential brand voice: Easy-going, helpful and conversational, but not too casual.

These answers – and this voice – might not work for your brand, but I hope you get the idea of how to begin defining your brand's voice.

The more unique your brand voice, the easier it should be for customers, advocates and others to feel connected to you. Isn't that better than everyone sounding the same?

But don't forget: No matter what your voice ends up being, be clear about what can and cannot be shared publicly and what information could go either way, depending on the situation. The biggest action step still remains: Start sharing stories.

Tone – even when defined – can be hard to hit

Keep in mind that your voice – even when well-defined and written deliberately, can sometimes be hard to read by our audiences. It takes practice, audience connection and consistency. Let's use email as an example. Probably everyone with access to email has been in this situation at one time or another:

One person's emails are always written in a snarky, negative or "I-know-better-than-you" tone. Always.

Why can't that person start writing in a nicer tone?

And then when you ask the writer about those emails, he or she says they weren't written in anything resembling a negative tone. In fact, he or she was smiling – nicely – when they were written. He was thinking his email would help the project move forward.

So why do we have such opposite viewpoints on the same emails? Sometimes people could pick better words. Or they could go into more depth to explain what they are talking about.

Seriously, the tone can't be detected in many of the emails we send. At all. The same can be true for social media postings and blogs. Let's take this simple email example "OK." Somebody emails those two letters back to acknowledge receiving an email. Maybe they meant: "Okkkayy, but that's a crazy idea." Maybe they gave permission. Or maybe there's another interpretation that the recipient can dream up.

And how come they didn't say something like, "OK, that's the best idea I've heard in my 49 years in business."

The room for interpretation is great and could be never ending. Maybe they meant the opposite. Stop it!

Often it goes back to the offline relationship of the people corresponding. If they get along well and work well together, chances are recipients won't detect any nasty tone. If there are offline issues, even the nicest emails end up being read with a negative connotation.

This is something to keep in mind as we are continuing text-based communication – publicly and one-on-one. There is one thing receivers can do here. We can read emails with a smile and give senders the benefit of the doubt.

How personal and business brands can interact

As more and people and businesses participate publicly in the Participation Age it's also important to remember and acknowledge that everyone is a brand. Everyone has been a brand. It's not a new concept, really, but with the birth of digital social media we are now calling it what it is.

There's three main brands in most people's lives.

- The people brand
- The business brand
- The leader brand

I've seen studies that say that more and more people will work as contractors and not full-time employees. More and more will be telecommuting. And even if everyone is working that way, people's brands, their clients' brands and others will still interact with each other.

The business brand

This one is easy. It's the business brand and related accounts. Company A is owned by its owners and shareholders. The accounts are clearly identifiable and have the business name on them. The business (let's hope) has a strategy and a person or team update this account in line with that strategy. Even business accounts should behave like people. It's more personable.

The leader brand

This is the first of two kinds of accounts that involves people as the public face. You may notice that I don't call them personal accounts. Having true personal accounts will become harder and harder as work and lives integrate more and more and become more open online.

Especially for leaders in an organization, it will be hard to see a difference between their "personal" and "professional" identities. If those two identities don't align, it's hard for employees and external audiences to align them with each other. One's trustworthiness could suffer.

And the notion that work is different from life isn't right anyway. People are what they are – whether it's when they get paid for a task or when they are at home playing with their kids. It's all part of the total person.

The people brand

I call these people brands instead of employee brands because it's less and less likely that people these days will work for the same company their entire career. I love where I currently work full time, but it's certainly not the only thing that defines me.

The people brands are company-independent, but when all three brands truly align internally and externally, that's when companies, their leaders and employees can all help each other by:

- Strengthening each other's brands
- Acquiring more customers

- Learning from each other
- Participating in our communities

Smart people build their own brands and then integrate them with the companies they lead or work for. Smart companies and leaders encourage that and even help the three circles work together authentically and transparently with simple rules outlined.

Where there might be a rub

In the past, I've heard about journalists and other communications professionals who have established their brand on social media, and then the organizations they work for claim they own those people's social media brands.

Baloney!

Usually, they just end up claiming that they were talking about "the accounts." Probably because it's hard to argue an organization owns a person's brand.

Typically, this is only a topic of discussion when an employee with a strong brand is leaving a company that was reaping benefit from that employee's strong personal brand. Instead of trying to hold on, maybe the company could have tried harder to keep that employee! What year is this?

On one side, there might be some truth that an organization helped an individual build his or her brand. But the brand also benefited from the person's individual brand. And what would an organization do with that person's accounts when that person leaves anyway? It's not like they can have somebody else take them over.

"Hi, I'm your new @ctrappe." That doesn't make any sense at all.

When these discussions happen, they are a holdover from a time when (some) business owners thought they could control everything. In a world of abundance, there's no reason we can't all have our own pieces, which can operate on their own at times and at other times come together and support each other.

When we all encourage individuality, community and authentic storytelling, we can fill our lives with meaningful experiences.

And when all these brands interact with each other authentically and pull in others, we have the start to an authentic community that is sharing meaningful stories. This is also where we can bring influencers into the mix. Sometimes those influencers are inside an organization and sometimes they are outside connections. Either way, connecting with them is useful and can build relevant connections.

Influencer marketing

Marketing to an influencer is one of the latest marketing trends. You need to reach a bunch of people in a certain demographic or interest group, so you go out and identify somebody to whom this particular group listens. You then reach out to this influencer and try to get him or her to share whatever it is you are selling with his or her followers.

If this exchange is mutually beneficial for all involved, there is likely nothing wrong with this relationship transaction. But focusing all of your energy on only the people who appear to be influencers is not authentic and is too narrow of a focus.

You might decide that some people are influencers because they have 100,000 followers on Twitter. Did you know that some people buy followers? There's a chance that somebody with that many followers perhaps has bought followers from another country who have nothing to do with your target audience.

Don't get me wrong. Some people have that many followers who are interested in what that person has to say. And they all follow voluntarily. For free.

There are ways to analyze somebody's followers and see if they might be your target audience and whether it's beneficial to connect with them.

It's also totally OK to connect with others who might be interested in what you have to say and who only have 23 followers on Twitter. Because offline, they likely influence many others. That's something we can't see from their Twitter numbers.

How many people do they influence offline? How vocal are they? They might be very loud about the products they love and the products they hate, and tell all of their friends, and even get their friends to continue spreading the same message. Ultimately, **everyone is an influencer to somebody**.

I influence my wife's decisions, and she influences mine and others. She isn't even on Twitter, so you can't get to her there, but you can reach her through me. But that's not necessarily as visible online as is finding somebody with 100,000 followers.

What's the answer to all this?

I think it's a mix. Yes, it's quite OK and necessary to identify and reach out to our target audiences (a.k.a. interested communities), wherever they might be.

It's also important to get the organizational story straight. It's no longer about shaping messages. It's about living our stories. Step 1 is that everyone lives the story first before we try to tell it.

- This is our organization's story. Here's why we exist (besides making money), and here's how we can help you (the members of the audience).
- We share that story in a mutually beneficial way for the audience and the organization.

It can be useful to analyze our delivery mechanisms, and it will help us reach more people when we identify the right channels. But like people constantly trying to manipulate search engine results in a way that's not authentic – like black hat search engine optimization – analyzing things goes only so far and can be time-consuming.

Plus, it's easy to get stuck in analysis paralysis, where we analyze so much that nothing else ever gets done.

Spend at least as much time – or more – on actually creating valuable content in which your target audiences might be interested. Or better yet, create content that helps them solve a problem and is a topic that aligns with your business mission and interests.

Sharing authentic solutions to problems establishes the author as an expert and potential thought leader. Eventually readers might decide to become customers. I've seen it happen. I only say "might" because if not done right, they won't.

Those readers, even if we don't know their names (yet) are likely influencers somewhere of somebody. If they consume our content, they likely have an opinion about us and might share it. Even if we can't measure it.

Don't change your story because of competitors

Once we get started sharing our authentic stories, it's good to remember that our stories are our stories – even if other people do not agree with them or have their own stories – both things that are likely to happen at some point. Stick with your story.

It can happen: A couple of competitors decided to be less authentic. Certainly, I won't change my approach because of that.

We want to win in whatever industry we are in. I do. Heck, one of my strengths is being competitive.

It's also easy to overanalyze what others are doing and then simply copy – or try to copy – what they are doing. What kind of life would it be if our purpose was just to copy what others are doing? It doesn't feel authentic and certainly is not unique to each person or organization.

I'm not talking about copying new techniques for content distribution. Networks change. User behavior sometimes changes.

It's good to keep up on those items and adjust from time to time. And one organization's best practices might not be another's.

Ultimately, the foundation of our stories and at some point our passions, doesn't change. The way we accomplish things might evolve. The tools certainly change. Our story is our story, though.

Yet copying from each other is an unfortunately common technique. The Internet is filled with useless, spammy, annoying marketing techniques. Much of it exists because people copy techniques from each other. Even when those techniques are annoying, they quickly are declared best practices – or at least practices that work, even though the definition of "working" is pretty low.

Example: People continue to sell to each other on social media because that's what a lot of people do. It works just well enough to make it feel successful.

Also: On social media, in e-newsletters and other channels, people make users click because the only way we think we can measure success is website traffic. For most organizations, clicks are embarrassingly low. I'd focus on other metrics: Engagement metrics that are actually showing some success.

There are plenty more annoying marketing techniques out there that are being deployed. You probably have your own list of pet peeves. When I ask people why they do whatever they are doing that is not the most user-friendly tactic, here's an answer I get often: That's what Brand A is doing, and I read that it's working for them.

Just because it's working for them doesn't make it a non-annoying technique that builds audiences long-term. And did they say what they meant by "working?"

I'm all for learning from each other, and there are many experts I learn things from. I quote them. I take their ideas and apply them to authentic storytelling to help you and I tell better, less markety stories.

But I certainly don't copy entire processes.

That wouldn't be unique to me, and it wouldn't feel very innovative. And I want to innovate. I want to create and be part of something worthwhile. Copying somebody who isn't even doing it right may sound easy, but it won't get me there long-term. It won't even get me started. It's actually a waste of time. The shortcut is the longer way.

I remember reading about a company a few years ago. They were known for calling and annoying people over dinner to get them to sign up for their service.

They were hated by many. So why did they do it? Because it worked just enough to make them a ton of money. Congratulations – today they are out of business.

Learn from others, but be super careful when you copy them. You might risk your reputation on it, and our reputation is really all you have long term.

Copying crap will just produce more crap.

But being unique is so hard – mostly because we keep saying that it is. It's really a mindset. Once we make up our mind to be unique and be what we are, it's actually quite easy. Start saying how easy it is and it'll be so.

Storytelling: We learn by doing

Before we know it there'll be a new tool that's worthwhile to use and that can help us share our stories. The tools change and evolve – so don't get so focused on the tools, but more on the art of storytelling. Then use the latest and most relevant channels and tools as they may apply.

Anyone can tell authentic stories. Seriously. As long as we make up our minds that we want to do that, it's possible.

I've seen it. People with no formal background in storytelling start becoming great public storytellers. That's the key with storytelling: It is very public.

I have started wondering how many potential storytelling rock stars ended up pursuing other career opportunities. There are probably some, maybe many. I hope not thousands or even more than that. But how would I know for sure? Yikes.

I do know this: I run across natural authentic storytellers all the time in many fields:

- Healthcare
- Customer service
- Computing
- Training
- And others

Some of these people have started to blog or are active on social media –in essence they are sharing their authentic stories, which is great. People don't have to be doing this full time to be great and impactful storytellers. Anyone can do it, really. It does help when you aren't doing it on top of a 50-hour a week job.

This leads me to wonder how we even decide which career path to follow. Is it mostly about what we stumble into? What our parents tell us to do, maybe? It certainly was kind of a stumble in my case.

In the 1990s as an 11-year-old boy, I was lifting weights at a gym in Germany where I ran into another lifter who had the best stories. I inquired, "How do you know all these things?"

Turns out that he was a journalist, and it was his job to find and then tell great stories. Awesome! That sounded like something I would want to do. I kind of stumbled into it. What if I had stumbled into a different path? Who knows if I would have been nearly as successful at it? Ha, did I just call myself successful?

For all the authentic storytellers out there, whether you are doing it as a full-time gig or you "stumbled into" doing a blog, never stop telling stories. Especially stories that people want to consume and that enlighten, inspire hope and share knowledge. If you haven't started, it's never too late to get going now.

Many of us, however, have lost the art of storytelling that we've had during our childhood. We don't share stories. We share statements, or we share an opinion or a marketing message: Please buy from me. Me! Me! Me! Click here. Did you click?

Or we tell and don't show. We make statements saying that something is great instead of giving specific examples of why it is great. Stories build relationships beyond transactions. Anyone can share stories. Anyone. But it takes time and practice. And, of course, some people have more of a natural talent than others.

Sometimes people ask me to give them the "secret formula" of how to tell stories. Ready? Here it is:

- Recognize a great story.
- Determine who might want to hear the story.
- Determine what details to share.
- Tell the story.

Done. It's really that simple. In theory, football is, too: Run a play the opponent can't defend, and you score – and ultimately win. Of course, playing football (and especially winning in football) takes a lot of practice, and even then, only a few people make it to the top levels.

It takes practice, ongoing practice. The same is true of storytelling. The concept might be relatively simple, but the practice and refinement is ongoing – like about anything in life.

How to write and share accurate stories

Sometimes people share things inaccurately by mistake. Other times, opinion was presented as fact. Sometimes it may have been shared inaccurately on purpose.

As brands (people, organizations, and businesses) are trying to connect online by sharing accurate stories, inaccuracies don't help. They hurt. Content moves quickly today, and people might forget one inaccurate statement. But it's usually harder and takes longer to (re)build credibility once that has happened.

Building credibility with an audience takes time. It's slow and steady. It can be lost quickly, though.

How do you know a story is accurate?

How do you know what's accurate, and how do you make sure you are sharing accurate stories? There are several ways:

Research reporting – You conduct research using credible sources and don't fidget with the facts. You report what you find through research. How do you know the sources are credible? Same concept. Choose sources that have built credibility over time.

Your experience – It's your first-person experience (and, again, you are sharing it honestly). Think of parent bloggers and others who are sharing their personal stories online. They are often believable because the stories shared are personal and appear to be truthful.

Your opinion – Straight-up opinion. You see something that relates to your blogging or content niche and offer an opinion. The key here is to say it's an opinion.

Your opinion based on research – Some opinions can't be accurate without research. For example, let's say you think a particular intersection is particularly dangerous. Thinking doesn't constitute knowing. Your opinion about that intersection can be told as a first-person story about what happened to you at that intersection. After you research public records about dangerous intersections, you can then deliver an opinion, backed up by research, about how dangerous it is.

More tips

Writing in your unique voice can help you differentiate yourself. Another way is to share authentic stories that don't constantly try to sell your reader something. A third approach concerns the words we choose.

Some things to consider about those words:

Questions. Questions can cause audience members to tune out. Let's say you ask: "Have you had issues with intersection ABC?" If the answer is no, the post's relevancy goes way down for that reader.

Use words that show and don't tell. Consider these two examples: "This product did not break under the weight of five men – 1,100 pounds. You don't have to worry that it will break if your baby sits on it." Or: "This is the most durable and best product for babies." Which one is more authentic, more powerful?

Don't guess. If you don't know for sure, don't guess.

Sharing accurate stories

It takes time to build a credible, multichannel content strategy that shares accurate stories all the time across different channels. But once your strategy is established, it can be beneficial for content producers as well as readers. We all can learn, grow and connect together through the sharing of accurate stories.

And don't assume things. It's OK to ask questions. I usually don't let people not responding to me stop me from publishing something, but I do ask questions to learn their actual intent.

The importance of being new

Audiences respond to new stories. But marketing and communications people ask me, "Why do we always have to create new content to share on our website and social media? Once it's all up and running, it's good, right?"

For some website content that does not change, that is true. No changes are necessary unless a fact changes.

In blogging and social media, new stories and content are important. People don't come back to blogs or social media networks to read the same thing over and over. They want new content – valuable, interesting or entertaining stories.

We pay attention to new things. Some people have said this is an instinct from when our ancestors had to be aware of wild animals. A new wild animal in your vicinity got your attention. It might try to eat you.

And while stories on social media don't present that kind of threat, the same concept applies. We pay attention to new things. And we especially pay attention to new things when they are relevant.

Think of instances when somebody starts sharing a story with a group. To some, the story might be new, and they will listen. Those in the group who have heard the story before probably will tune out. "I already know this." The person sharing the story might even acknowledge the people who have already heard the story – stop me if you've heard this, they'll say.

Think of how exciting it is to share something new with people who haven't heard it. We bond over the experience.

If you fly with any regularity, how often do you still listen to the flight attendant announcements? They all read the same script (for the most part). That's why it's news when a flight attendant changes it up some. People even take their phones out to shoot video and post it on YouTube or Facebook.

That's because it's something new. It entertains us. Sometimes it enlightens us. When new things are irrelevant, though, they still will be ignored by many.

New content that is relevant helps us stay relevant with our audiences. Since there are new things going on in our lives, businesses and organizations, creating and sharing new stories is possible.

To do this, we need to capture new stories as they happen and then share them. Our audiences will thank us.

Tell stories through people

Sharing new things through stories is great. What makes it powerful is sharing those new things through people – or the impact the new things had on people.

We've all seen the stories where this wasn't done.

Here's a new piece of technology that's going to be doing X, Y or Z. In healthcare, the new technology might save somebody's life or improve their quality of life.

Unfortunately, many stories continue to tell and not show. As I've said many times: Great storytellers show. They don't tell.

The difference between the two:

Telling: This device makes breathing easier for people who have had Condition A and undergo this procedure.

Showing: Susan, 56, was easily out of breath from just holding her infant grandson. She's been suffering from Condition A and is one of the first in the United States to get this new device. Today, she plays with her grandson, climbs stairs and feels much better. "This surgery gave me my life back," she says. "I can finally breathe again."

This is a made-up example, but I'm sure you get the point.

Why is showing so much harder than telling? Because getting the details takes time.

Telling is easier, but showing is more effective and more relatable to audiences. Taking the time to show will pay off long-term. Audiences will love you for it and, in some industries, it's a differentiator because everyone else is continuing to tell.

With all our technology, we still relate to people.

Attention is earned

Once we share our truly unique and authentic stories, we have a shot at getting people's attention. Attention can be worth more than money. But when you earn attention, it can lead to more money through additional customers.

Think of young children. They demand attention, and often – at least when they are little – demand it by being cute or by accomplishing a first (the six-month-old who just rolled over, the six-year-old who just read a book).

We pay attention for four reasons:

- We have a relationship with our children.
- We have a connection with them and want to see what they are doing.
- We have hopes and dreams for them.
- We're interested in the newness of what they are doing. When our children do something new, we don't want to miss it. Think of the disappointed parents who miss a first because they were traveling.

Why is this relevant?

What's happening around us impacts us. Let's take the six-month-old starting to crawl. Yes, it's new and she's our daughter, but even if those two things weren't the case, the crawling might still have relevance to us. We'd better pay attention to make sure she crawls around safely.

Sometimes people think they can demand attention. For some people this is possible. But mostly only in the short term.

Think of an angry boss demanding attention. He might get it, but as soon as you escape his attention, you might be updating your resume and looking for a new job.

How does longer-lasting attention happen? It happens by sharing information that people want to consume, that helps them solve a problem or that educates them.

Brands jumping into content marketing, blogging or social media should not even try to demand attention. Work on earning it.

Once attention is earned, people remember your stories and events and can even tell your story to others. Earned attention leads to advocacy.

8-second attention span: What it means

People's attention spans are around eight seconds. Eight seconds. That's short. Hello? Are you still reading?

What does that time span mean to content marketers and authentic storytellers? Does it mean content should be short? Consumable in eight seconds total? That would be around the length of a Tweet or something close to it.

While it's possible to tell stories in Tweets, not all content needs to be that short. I love Twitter, but I also read books. Sometimes in hardcover format and sometimes on my Kindle app.

What do all the great books and Tweets have in common? They continuously regenerate our interest in them.

I've seen Tweets that put me to sleep. Usually it's the ones that use every single character and abbreviate words to the point it makes reading difficult and less than enjoyable.

I've also seen books that assume readers will stick around. They drag on, are verbose and hide facts in complex sentence structures. Some people might read them – because they have to, I assume.

What the eight-second attention span means to content marketers and storytellers is that we have to earn the attention of our audience every eight seconds. We have to say something – or at least foreshadow something – to keep people's attention.

Sometimes that can be a new fact, something surprising or even a picture. During a presentation to a live audience, it might be a change in the presenter's tone of voice or a deliberate physical movement.

Either way, the eight-second attention span doesn't mean all stories need to be told completely in eight seconds. It means we need to earn attention every eight seconds.

Certainly some stories can be completely told in eight seconds or even in two seconds. But we don't have to undermine the value of complete storytelling just because people's attention span is eight seconds.

Give the story the length it needs to be told correctly and in a way that's engaging.

Be concise: You can cut facts

While stories can be on the long side when they deserve it, we also can cut facts and unnecessary wording to keep things concise. Edit like you are running out of words.

Content marketers, storytellers and even executives can fall in love with the facts of a story they are sharing with a wider audience. Don't be married to every word – just because it's yours.

"If we love them, our audiences will, too," might be the attitude. That's not always the case. Sometimes cutting facts is a necessity.

Not all facts are created equal, and some don't add much to the flow of a story or inform a specific audience. But cutting facts and details can be hard.

First of all, we might be so close to the story that it's hard to see that Fact A is not nearly as important as Fact B and doesn't add much to the story. Leaving it in, however, can turn away an audience that is getting bored by unnecessary content.

These facts and nuggets of content can come as pieces of writing, audio recordings and even video.

The amount of work it takes to cut facts on these different media varies, but it can be done on all. For example, cutting content in a written piece is, technically speaking, easier than cutting it in video. With text on the screen in a word processing system, text can be cut in seconds. What text to cut, however, can be a longer decision-making process.

Cutting facts on audio and video takes a bit more work. Audio files take longer to save than a text document. And depending on what's being cut, the editor might have to work around words bleeding over each other. Depending on the speaker's pace, it can be hard to cut content.

Video editors can face the same barrier and more. A lot of times B-roll needs to be used when what a speaker says is cut apart. That way, the video doesn't show how sentences are being cut apart. That could create a bad user experience for the viewer.

Saving, rendering and exporting takes additional time. And then the new file still needs to be reviewed.

It's OK to keep content concise and clear and to spend the time to make sure our stories engage our audiences. But it's also good to keep in mind that this process takes time and adds time to a project.

Knowing when to cut content

When unnecessary content is shared, it's usually obvious to the consuming audience. Yawn.

"Why is this being shared?" is not the reaction we are looking for. Keep in mind that many people are short on time but will make time for content that engages them, content they care about and that solves a problem for them.

Several steps have worked for me over the years as a traditional and brand journalist as well as a content marketer.

Really weigh each fact that's being included. Why do I need this? Am I sharing it in the most meaningful and most understandable way?

Ask somebody else to review your story. Ask them for feedback. Were they engaged during the whole piece? If not, ask them when they were "bored."

If you can, let your story **sit for a few days and then come back with fresh eyes** to see what you might be able to cut.

Instead of simply cutting facts and pieces of the story, start by cutting words. Take a look at each word, and cut the words that are unnecessary.

An example:

- This also will help content be clearer and more concise.
- This helps content be clear and concise.

The end goal of the stories we share isn't about us – the storytellers – expressing ourselves or even writing for ourselves. It's about the audience. Most audience members today have little time. Keeping stories as concise as possible helps us connect to our readers. Cut facts and pieces of content that don't add much. Keep the ones that share the stories in the most meaningful way.

Is our audience internal or external?

Defining our audience helps us make the stories we share more relevant to that target audience. That's another way to know what content to cut and what to leave.

Most organizations have external audiences of consumers (people who might buy things from them), customers (people who have bought things from them) and advocates (people who spread their message). Sometimes audience members move back and forth between the roles.

The most successful content marketers define their audience at a much more granular level. For example:

- Moms with young children
- Divorced dads
- Traditional marketers trying to make it in a new media world
- Young adults who are overweight and are looking for weight-loss tips

Did you notice who is not listed here?

- Your boss
- Your boss' boss
- The guy down the hall at your office who is looking for a new job but who gets to vote on new publications

"But, but, but," you might say, "of course, my boss is the audience. He approves this stuff and reads it like he's the audience." Even when he's not.

Unfortunately, that's a reality in many organizations, and it can be a problem. When we produce content for internal audiences and then present it to external audiences like it's actually for them, the external audience – the one that ultimately might buy from us – suffers. Such "vetted" content might be unappealing, not compelling and, at the worst, irrelevant. Often it ends up being marketing speak-filled crap.

Sorry, bosses, many times you are not your organization's target audience.

This can be hard to remember, understand and ultimately verbalize to the team once you – the boss – are buying in. Bosses who understand this concept ask before reviewing anything, "Who is your audience?" They might even add, "Because it isn't me."

Sound hard? It is. Why? There are several reasons.

Some bosses are used to being right – even when they aren't.

And, more importantly, it's hard to think about audiences that might be slightly different from us.

Let's say I'm the CEO of a business. I'm kind of an early adopter and integrate the latest tools into my life. My family's, too. They sometimes even love it.

Customers of my business describe themselves as lower middle class. Many barely make ends meet, but they have spending money from time to time. Few are early adopters.

It should be easy to see that I have to set aside my own interests when evaluating content and stories for the actual audience. That's the only way to create content that will be relevant and worthwhile to them.

How do we get there? We need great storytellers and great bosses who empower their teams to tell an organization's stories for their actual audiences – stories that are compelling, educational and (start to) build long-term relationships.

It starts with the top. Of course, we also have to remember to not change authentic stories to marketing stories. Here's what actually happened. Here's what a good marketing brochure would sound like. That's always a danger, too. Usually, those changes are not state-of-the-art innovation.

How to write a good headline

Let's discuss how to write a good, authentic headline. Headlines are one of the more important pieces of our shared stories, especially on blogs. The story also needs to keep the promise of the headline, so we can't overpromise what the article will deliver, but we do have to make it engaging.

Writing a good headline is crucial in getting an audience's attention – the humans and the search engines, which bring more humans. If the headline doesn't get somebody's attention in the first few seconds, the person might move on to read something else, not necessarily because they wouldn't have cared about our content, but they didn't know they cared because the headline was vague.

Writing a good headline: Get to the point

I've written and edited thousands of web posts going back to the days of Eastern Iowa News. My thoughts on this topic are based on trial and error, web traffic reviews and research done by others that I've reviewed.

Web headlines are different from newspaper headlines. Newspaper headlines sometimes play with words. For the web, it's usually better to get to the point. Be clear and concise. Don't make the user guess what's being written about.

That's true for a couple of reasons:

- Web users move quickly. If they don't understand a headline, they move on. Don't lose them on a word play or reference that is vague or doesn't resonate.
- It won't help with search engines. Google and other engines understand a headline that says, "How to write a headline for the web." Search engines won't get "Webby Headlines" or something like that.

Tips for writing a good headline

Writing a good headline comes down to **clarity** and, to a degree, **brevity**. **Accuracy** also is important. The headline needs to reflect the content of the post.

When writing a headline, think about the main points of the post. Try to use keywords in the headline. To take this a step further you could do a keyword search on Google and pick keywords that are more likely to be used by searchers. Log into Google Adwords to use the keyword planner.

I see headlines every day like this: "Today's Links" or "Today's Advertising News" or something equally vague. Is that really the most relevant headline? It's better to pick something more relevant out of the content and highlight that, or summarize the overall theme (if there is one). Those headlines likely work – or appear to work - for some established brands, but I wouldn't recommend starting there.

In the past, I've also used the headline as almost the first sentence of the article. The headline kicks it off and the article flows from there. That's a bit different from how headlines were handled when I was in the newspaper world from 1999 to 2007. Reporters wrote the stories. Somebody else put the headline on after that. In this new way of publishing, the headline can become part of the post.

Also remember what the message is that you are trying to get across. For example, if I send an email to my family with vacation photos, I may be able to title it "Christoph's Vacation Photos," and they likely will look at it. But that wouldn't be the best headline for a blog that covers communication-related topics. This one would be better: "Lessons learned while shooting vacation pictures with my iPhone." Granted, that will be a very different post from just uploading my vacation pictures, but it will be more relevant to an audience that cares about content creation and related tools.

Writing relevant, timeless web content

With all this content creation you will be doing, it's also important to make content last as long as possible. It's certainly OK to offer unique opinions about current news events from time to time. But it's also important to share content that has a longer relevancy.

Every once in a while, an expert in one thing or another will tweet a link to an older blog post that's relevant to a current topic. It's timeless content for the web. A lot of times others who are mentioning it on their streams mention that it's from a year or two ago.

A lot of times, the post is indeed timely once again. But many times, had the post been written in what I call non-time-sensitive language, it would be even more relevant today because you wouldn't be thinking about the time element (oh, yeah, this is old).

Blog posts aren't newspaper articles. Much content is timeless and is as relevant two years from now as it is today. But it can be hard not to use time-sensitive words or phrases in writing or even while speaking on a podcast or video.

Some examples of this kind of time-stamp language:

- Today
- Today on December 1, 2015
- For the next thirty days
- Right now

You can cut many of these time references from newly created materials. It often doesn't matter **when** you wrote about an issue. It does matter at times in print journalism when people read a newspaper. It's supposed to be about current events. Blogs don't have to be.

Much of the content that organizations create is not time-sensitive. Some things are, of course, but most content isn't.

A piece on how a project teaches skills that help people in the ever-changing world and workforce can – and should – stay relevant for a while. At least until somebody decides the specific skill mentioned in the story is no longer taught.

I saw a video from 2004 in 2013, and it had interviews discussing a specific organization. Much of what they said in the video was still relevant in 2013 and probably will be in the future. If you don't look at the quality of the video (it's not HD) and nobody told you that it was from 2004, you would never know based on the content alone.

In the online world, it's much more user-friendly to use the actual date as opposed to today, tomorrow or yesterday. I've heard of some online editors say those words are used to show immediacy and are later changed. But I've never actually seen a site where they **are** later changed. I have seen plenty of sites where "tomorrow" was actually a week ago.

So, why doesn't everyone write this way? Because it's not the traditional way we are taught to write.

It's much easier to write "today" as opposed to finding another term. Or perhaps better: Remembering to find a different term.

How do you change it? Here's what has worked for me:

- Recognize why it needs to change and when.
- Think of your audience. For example, if your piece is a one-hit wonder, and you are wishing people a happy holiday, it's OK to use time-sensitive language. The message won't make sense in March anyway. But if it's a piece that can (and should) still have relevance in March, pick other words. Of course, holiday posts can be re-promoted every year for that year's holiday season, so be careful with date references.
- Execute: Take a moment, think, and pick other words. Rework content when necessary.

Words to avoid using online

With responsive design, RSS, mobile and so many different devices with different screen sizes out there, there are some additional words to avoid when writing for online audiences.

The reason is things move around, depending on how readers are viewing your content. On desktop the picture might be to the right of the paragraph, but on mobile phones it might be above it. It's another thing to think about when we produce content, I know. Hey, nobody said this would be easy.

Avoid using these words in web content:

"Pictured at right/below"

Depending on the site's design and the user's device, the picture might not be at right but instead below or even above. My blog uses responsive design, and pictures show differently on different devices.

Using this kind of descriptive language also doesn't work as nicely if posts are automatically fed into an email newsletter. The post might say "the picture below," but email readers actually have to click over to the website to see the picture and the rest of the post.

Solution: Don't use the phrases. Use self-explanatory pictures and/or add a caption/cutline. Don't even call out the photos in the copy. They should work without saying "at right."

"After the jump"

I don't see this all that often anymore. This phrase means the story continues after clicking on a link. It comes from the newspaper industry where stories "jumped" from the front page to an inside page. I could probably write an entire book on how unfriendly that is to readers even in the newspaper world. Maybe later.

These words make sense if readers are visiting a site's homepage. But they don't work on RSS feeds or if somebody has a direct link to the article.

Solution: Avoid using it all together.

“As mentioned above”

I usually notice this in books (on my iPad Kindle), when the author says this and whatever is supposed to be “above” is actually on a previous page.

Solution: Say “as mentioned earlier” or avoid using it completely.

Words matter, including in our online blog posts. As devices continue to evolve, it’s important for us – the content producers – to consider how our chosen words add value to our consumers.

If we say to check out the picture below, but it’s not below, that doesn’t add value.

What’s the right length for content?

Gathering all this great content, of course, leads us to the question of how long content should be. The length of something – a speech, a presentation, a blog post, a movie, a book – doesn’t necessarily determine its quality.

But sometimes we default to thinking that it does.

I remember being invited to speak at a global conference in a 15-minute time slot. I mentioned this to one person, and she said, “Only 15 minutes? Is that worth going for?”

I suppose it depends on our definition of “worth it,” but a good, compelling, relevant story can be shared in 15 minutes. Absolutely.

TED and TEDx Talks – those inspiring videos recorded at conferences around the globe – are often under 15 minutes. And many of them rock.

Some people share great stories in Tweets at 140 characters or less, while some Tweets are useless marketing dribble. Some people write long, compelling books while some books can't be finished.

Instead of focusing on an artificial length, give a story the amount of time or length it actually needs. That takes discipline, the willingness to cut less important facts and the ability to keep refining.

No matter the medium, cut words like you are running out of them. If a word or fact doesn't add anything, cut it.

Share what needs to be shared to get your point across. Sometimes that's a Tweet and sometimes it might be a 1,000-word article.

Scheduling without driving yourself crazy

To distribute content use the scheduling tools that are available. We can't be online 24/7, afterall.

Every once in a while, people don't agree that authenticity goes together with the scheduling of posts and social media updates.

Why? Apparently, they believe authenticity can only happen when it's live.

With the kind of content I share and the way I share it, timing has nothing to do with authenticity. At all. Whether I share it now or later doesn't affect the genuine thought behind the post or update. Plus, global audiences never sleep, but we have to at some point.

Most of the things I publish have no time element. They are as relevant two weeks from now as when they were written. Of course, when I have something timely to say, I will publish it immediately. But that doesn't happen all that often. Most of my thoughts aren't tied to the current moment. Take this book, for example, most of the chapters are made up of previously written blog posts. I had to do some rewriting, adding of transitions but in general the content still worked, because it wasn't tied to the moment.

And when people respond to my scheduled posts, I respond as quickly and authentically as possible. The opinions I share in a scheduled update don't change in the time between the writing and the publishing. And when they do from time to time, I just acknowledge it. Not a big deal, really.

I have had it happen that somebody reading a scheduled Tweet asked for an example of the scenario mentioned. Due to the time that has passed, I couldn't remember one. In that case, my Tweet was still authentic and accurate. I just couldn't continue the discussion. That is clearly a downside to scheduling updates.

Audiences on social media networks, your blogs and other channels all appreciate meaningful, timely, relevant content. Some communication strategists have said that all channels should get unique content, but with the number of channels now available,

I've found this isn't the most effective strategy. It's nearly impossible to do really.

I advocate the **Create Once Publish Everywhere** strategy. Typically, I recommend starting with a blog post on a website and then distributing the reformatted content on other channels.

It's a good idea for your content strategy to include ideas and even steps to ensure all channels are included. You might make a checklist on your computer or on paper to make sure that happens.

Scheduling content: The why

Social media and blog posts can be published instantaneously. We have something to say, we write it (social or elsewhere), reread it (I hope!) and then publish or tweet it. #Done.

As part of a professional or advanced content strategy, I don't recommend that you publish things the second they are ready. Some content, of course, must go live immediately. For example, if something extremely timely needs to be tweeted, tweet it. Live. If somebody is asking a question on social media, respond.

But for produced stories that aren't related to current news events, I recommend scheduling content – the blog posts and related social media updates – with some time in between stories.

Here are the reasons for this strategy:

- A blog post might be finished at 2 a.m., but that might not be the best time to publish it. It can be hard to know the best time to publish a post. My tip: Experiment with different times and days, and watch web traffic and audience engagement. Repeat what works and build on that.

- You were able to pull 15 Tweets out of that blog post. You surely wouldn't want to post them all at once, especially if it's 2 a.m.
- Scheduling updates can make your brand appear much more active and engaged.
- Scheduling updates a ways out can make content production less stressful. No need to worry about tomorrow. We are working on pieces to be published three or more weeks from now.
- It assures that different stories don't "step on" each other.

A note of caution: Keep abreast of what is publishing when and what else is going on in the world and with your target audiences. You wouldn't want an unrelated post accidentally be connected negatively to a breaking news event.

When to respond to breaking news

On the other hand, it's totally OK to respond to the discussion surrounding breaking news and insert yourself through your blog and social media.

Some people call this "news jacking," which sounds kind of negative to me, so I don't use that term.

When you insert yourself it should be about adding something meaningful and useful to what's going on out there in the world and is being reported through (traditional) news media.

It can look like this:

- You hear about a news event.
- You decide you have something to say about it in addition to what's been reported. Restating it or saying "I agree with that" doesn't add much value.
- You publish a blog post and distribute and reformat your "two cents worth" through social media posts.

Sharing such perspectives can lead to a good-sized audience paying attention and sometimes can earn media coverage. The event is already top of mind for many people.

To get to any kind of outcome – just as with any kind of blogging and authentic storytelling– the content you share has to be:

- Informational
- Educational
- Thought-providing
- Not promotional

Depending on the breaking news situation, it also can totally backfire. It's best to avoid blogging about tragedies, unless you have some true expertise to share.

I'm a fan of responding to breaking news when we can do it in a way that's meaningful to our audiences and non-promotional.

Some things to consider before deciding to participate:

- Why do you want to comment?
- What's in it for the organization?
- Are there any obvious drawbacks?
- What unique angle can you offer?

- Is the author prepared to talk to the media?
- Are you prepared to answer people's questions? That doesn't mean we have to prepare answers to 5,000 possible questions. It means we must be aware that people might have questions and that we are willing to answer them.
- Can you write and publish your content quickly? Let's say, in the next two hours? I can do that on my blog, but I write the article and then approve it. I do not go through a 22-step Approval Hell process.

Sharing our knowledge and expertise is what content marketing and authentic storytelling is all about. That can be during a breaking news event or during regular, weekly blog posts. Either way, it's about adding value. Content marketers sell without selling by providing useful, timely information.

Adding valuable information to breaking news events can be part of a content marketing plan.

Scheduling content: The tools

I recommend a self-hosted WordPress install for just about any content-heavy site. Using WordPress allows you to schedule posts to be published on a particular day and at a specific time. Instead of pushing PUBLISH, use the schedule function. Plus WordPress gives you an easy overview on the dashboard of upcoming scheduled posts.

By using the free Jetpack plugin on WordPress, you can easily tie your site to all of your social media accounts. An automatic update will go out once the post is published. Keep in mind this is just the headline with a link back to the post.

In addition, we should reformat content for each specific social network. Posts with links shouldn't be the only posts going out on your social media.

Look at the post's content again and pull individual social media updates out of it. These could be complete sentences lifted from the post or concepts addressed that you rewrote as a social media update.

Here's an example: Let's take the previous paragraph. Tweets from that could be:

- Don't just tweet links. Engage where the audience is. #socialmedia
- We reformat content based on users' expectations. They wouldn't expect any less. #ux #contentstrategy

Just one paragraph got me a couple more Tweets. You can repeat this a few times with each blog post.

All channels' audiences have different expectations, and channels display content differently. Keep this in mind as you are moving content between channels.

There are a number of social media scheduling tools out there. I recommend Hootsuite. It's free with premium options available and works well from desktop browsers as well as from mobile devices. Once you have Twitter, Facebook and LinkedIn accounts set up, sign up on Hootsuite.com to get a Hootsuite account. You can manage all of your social media accounts in Hootsuite and schedule posts from one central location. Still, make sure different networks get slightly different updates. Don't just send the same things to all networks because it's easy to do so.

Socialoomph.com charges a fee, but allows you to set tweets to repeat on a schedule. Very helpful.

Website or blog

Blog posts typically should be at least 300 words. That's helpful for search engines and also makes visitors' time worthwhile. Very few bloggers can pull off extremely short content that's worth reading. Short content, though, might work well on Twitter.

Email newsletters

Like all channels, testing what works is important here, too. One strategy you might try could include posting one main article in its entirety and then offering links to other headlines. Of course, a longer version of the main article was previously published on your website.

Social media

Twitter is short and continual (but don't post more than once every 15 minutes). You probably don't want to post that often to Facebook. Maybe 1-2 per day. With changes in Facebook reach you probably want to promote one or so posts per week – even if it's just for $25. LinkedIn is somewhere in the middle.

The key takeaway: Take bits and pieces of blog content and repurpose them as standalone pieces. Don't always link back to the blog. But link when it's relevant from time to time.

If you have enough content for social media, I suggest doing one post in the morning, one over the lunch hour and one around dinner time to get started. You can fill in posts in between as needed. As long as posts are relevant, audiences will appreciate them.

Overall, scheduling has helped me think through my thoughts and schedule authentic updates. Scheduling may be less timely, but it's more efficient and audience friendly as posts are spread out.

Even with scheduling, responding quickly is still important. The way we respond and at what speed also can be indicators of how truly authentic our answers are. When we take weeks to respond to an email, weigh our answer over and over, redraft it and get it approved by 14 people, how authentic is that?

Not very. It sounds like the time when organizations worked on their exact marketing message – the way they wanted to come across, as opposed to the way things actually were. Yes, some still do this.

Don't get me wrong. Some responses do take time, but in the meantime, we can send an intermediate response and say we received the email, will check into it and will be in touch as soon as possible. Of course, we can't forget about the promised follow-up.

Immediate responses help build relationships. People know they are being heard. For example, think of when a supervisor responds immediately to a team member by saying something is OK or that it's not going to work. At the very least, the lines of communication are open, and people know what's going on and that they're being heard. That is very important, so why don't we respond immediately?

Sometimes it's a time management issue. Let's say somebody has 10,000 followers on Twitter with a lot of engagement going on. Let's say this is an organization and that the time commitment to respond to all these people is quite high. Still, it's important. Sometimes it could be that we don't know what to respond or we don't have actual authority to respond.

The latest studies in 2015 say that people expect a response in one hour. I don't know if that is because most brands actually take much longer than that and consumers have lowered their expectations. I think our expectation for a response is much closer to the15-minute mark, which is what previous studies mentioned as an expectation point.

We can automate some responses, but for the most part, automatic messages on Twitter usually seem irrelevant and annoying to me. People – usually after I just followed them – send messages like this:

Thanks for following. Please also connect on Facebook/Instagram/LinkedIn and like my YouTube video here. (Or something along those lines.)

Others would ask questions: What's the current marketing problem you are trying to solve?

I find the direct messages that invite me to another network annoying. I'm already connected with you on Twitter and don't really know you yet. Why do I need to connect with you on LinkedIn right now?

Annoying marketing techniques will continue until they stop working.

But the abundance of direct message got me wondering: Maybe this technique does work. Then I wondered: How could I measure "working"? If I included a link, I could measure impact on the site.

I decided to add an automatic direct message, one that I hoped wasn't too annoying. It says: Thanks for connecting. I hope you'll check out my blog at AuthenticStorytelling.net.

I signed up for Crowd Fire and turned on its automatic direct messaging feature. I simply clicked on Automate and added a new Auto DM Marketing message. Easy enough.

I let it run for a while (and it's still running, as of this writing). It has helped with traffic to my blog, and I haven't seen any huge increase in unfollows on Twitter (I now have more than 40,000 followers.)

I've also seen an increase in e-newsletter subscriptions on my blog. Some I could track back to this tactic.

Interestingly, I also received a lot of positive feedback in the form of direct-reply messages. A number of people commented on how much they enjoyed the stories. Others told me they signed up for my e-newsletter – which means they'll receive every new blog post in their email. They definitely don't want to miss a thing – more loyal readers. Yay.

In theory, automated messaging seems to be an annoying tactic – and I'm certain it is to some – but it also has converted social media followers to blog readers. I've seen enough positive response to continue it, at least until it stops working. Automation can work great when the information presented is relevant to the person receiving it.

But, as I said before, responding in the moment is important. I was reminded of the power of rapid response when I rated an Uber driver three stars out of five and commented there were used tissues in the back seat. Almost immediately, I received an email from Uber letting me know it would address the issue. Then when I took an Uber in Mumbai, I rated the driver five stars and left a comment saying the service was great. Immediately, I received an email thanking me and letting me know about the struggles Uber is facing in Mumbai. It would be appreciated if I could tweet about my experience and sign a petition to keep Uber in Mumbai. Of course. They caught me at the right time.

Of course, it all takes time

I hear it often. People say they don't have time to share their stories – especially when it comes to sharing them on a blog.

Really, it's not about having the time, but making the time. I don't have the time either. I make it.

From the technology side of things, it's easy to blog from many places today. The WordPress mobile app, for example, lets you blog from your mobile device. I use it all the time. I'm writing 10 minutes here and there. Some posts (300 to 400 words) can be done in 25 minutes.

This is a picture of me typing out a post while cuddling with my 5-month-old daughter. Sometimes I paused to look at her. The post was done before she woke up. It's possible!

What about typing with one finger? Sure, it takes some getting used to. But learning and getting used to it is better than moving my daughter and parking myself in front of an actual computer.

What about the approval process for organizational blogging? Just because posts have to get approved doesn't mean they can't be written anywhere or anytime. Just save them as a draft or, if WordPress is completely integrated, save them as “pending approval” so the reviewer knows the post is ready for review.

Social media and blog strategies

Social media – like Twitter, Facebook, blogs, etc., - will not go away anytime soon. This section discusses some more tips and tricks on how to use networks effectively to share your stories and participate in a meaningful way. While I mention some specific networks throughout, these concepts pretty much apply no matter the network. They most certainly will change at some point.

Tell stories in the first person

Some of us sometimes forget that social media should be a personal and social communications tool. Yes, brands can be personal. So can people. But sometimes we forget that – probably in part because we were taught not to write in such a personal and conversational tone.

Third person in social media

I still see people and brands use third person in their own posts. If I posted in third person, it might look like this: ".@ctrappe received an award today and will speak at such and such event."

My guess is that this is a holdover from the "good old' days" of news release writing. Organizations and people routinely referred to themselves in the third person because they weren't necessarily supposed to be conversational or social. On social media, that holdover is just strange.

That Tweet is much better and more personal written like this: "I'm so excited to win this award and speak at this event. Hope to see you there."

I frequently compare social media to a dinner party, and we certainly wouldn't talk about ourselves in the third person at a dinner party.

I see that organizational accounts sometimes have to refer to others in the organization, and that's OK, but it's a far cry from this news release-type third person language. An airline might say, "Please let a crew member on your flight know" (after hearing about an issue). Even most airlines use first person in their Tweets.

Or a hospital might say, "Please DM us, and we will forward your information to the appropriate department" (after getting a question that needs an answer from a subject matter expert).

That's different from just talking about ourselves in the third person as a matter of routine.

Quoting others without quoting them

While we are talking about social media best practices, let's talk about quoting others. Some days I wonder where we used to find inspirational quotes before social media. Ha. Everyone is sharing their favorite quotes from dead and living people on all channels of social media.

Some people, I've noticed, quote articles or people without using quotation marks. That can cause confusion. Even when we link back to a full article that explains the source, quoting without credit on social media is confusing and borders on rude. Many social media users don't even click on those links. People (rightfully so) might expect that the post is from you, because, well, it came from you.

When we use other people's words, let's make sure to put quotation marks around them and name them as the source. If on Twitter, use their handle. On Facebook, tag them.

Quoting yourself

Other times, I've seen people quote themselves.

For example, consider this Tweet as an example:

"Quoting yourself is strange." – @ctrappe

If you share that, you are quoting me. That's fine (and appreciated). It's the appropriate way of quoting somebody. If I share that exact same Tweet, though, I'm quoting myself, and that's just strange and not conversational. It's OK – even recommended – to share other people's stories, as long as they are something your audience might care about.

Bad practices creep into everything. Some other pet peeves that I've stumbled across on Twitter are these:

- Only posting teasers and links.
- Tweeting who followed you to all your followers.
- Thanking everyone who RT'ed you in one Tweet.
- Back-to-back posts within seconds of each other.
- Back-to-back posts that all have links.
- Sending Facebook posts to Twitter and linking to Facebook for more.
- Tweets with two links.

- Too many hashtags in a single Tweet that make the Tweet unreadable.
- Egg head for profile photo. Please add an updated photo that reflects what you look like.
- Those "My week on Twitter. 12 new followers …" Tweets.
- Tweets with photos that link to Instagram.
- Tweets that use text speak.
- Tweets that try to share too much information and end up not making any sense.

Some of these might be OK with some audiences while they turn off other audiences, but let's keep in mind that social media is called social for a reason. It's supposed to be a conversation. Be personable, real and talk like humans would. It shouldn't be that difficult since we all are human.

What's with all these links on social media?

Some days I look at my Twitter stream and every single Tweet is asking me to click on a link for more information on whatever topic the Tweet mentioned.

Given that stories can be told in Tweets, there's really no need to link all the time. I link on Twitter, too. But not all the time. Twitter is the No. 1 social media outlet through which people find their way to my Authentic Storytelling blog. So it's surely tempting to link more. I want more people on my blog.

On social media, I like to advocate the 60-30-10 formula of sharing:

- 60 percent of posts should be content without links in which we just share soundbites and other self-contained native content.
- 30 percent should be responding to and re-sharing other people's content.
- 10 percent can include links to more.

I also want to reach more people who care about what I care about. Making them hop from one social network to somewhere else is not going to help me build those relationships. People, for the most part, engage where they are. Just figure out how to measure the engagement there instead of making them jump somewhere else.

This is especially true when we think of social media as a dinner party. Social media is about conversation. At a dinner party, we talk and connect. We don't say: "For the rest of the story, please visit my website tomorrow."

Is all this linking working anyway? It all depends on what the definition of "working" is. If 2 percent of followers click, you lose 10 followers and gain 12 for a net of 2 new followers, some might consider that working. I'm not so sure.

We also can look at referrals to a site. From social media, Twitter has sent the most traffic to my blog. But search engines drive more traffic than Twitter and Facebook combined.
What's the right answer? I think it comes down to a mix. It's OK to link to new blog posts – especially when they dive deeper into what you normally talk about on social media. The audience will

appreciate more depth. But make sure not to link on every single social media update.

Also keep in mind that content starts to spread when others start sharing it. Make sure it's easy for others to share the content from your website. Adding share buttons is easy enough. And WordPress and other content management systems now allow you to insert pre-written social media suggestions, where you can suggest people tweet a short excerpt from your blog. I use the Click to Tweet plugin on my WordPress blog for this.

To link or not to link on social media? It's an important question to ponder to maximize engagement, connections and transactions. It's a fine line between sharing valuable content and using social media as only a link-delivery system.

The importance of growing your audience

If nobody sees our great authentic stories, did they happen?

Yes, but too few people saw them, so it's important to grow your audience.

Here's an example from Twitter:

Twitter is a great network to connect with like-minded people and those who care about the things you want to talk about. The more relevant the connections you make, the better for everyone.

There are different ways to grow followers.

Some people try to sell 5,000 followers for $29, and while they might be delivered, these followers may have no interest in what you are talking about. At all. Additionally, buying followers isn't very authentic. If you talk a lot, you likely will lose them quickly anyway. Save your money and take the family out for a meal.

But the larger the relevant audience we can assemble, the more impact we can have and, in the long term, the more impact that can have on our businesses.

So how do you grow a Twitter following in a meaningful, authentic way?

I gained about 20,000 followers on Twitter in just two years. Here's how I did it:

- **Connecting** – I connect with people whose updates I want to follow. Some days – like on weekends – I follow hundreds of people. Many of them follow me back. If I find their Tweets interesting, I stay connected. If they continuously do one of my Twitter pet peeves, I unfollow them. It's not about you. It's about me not liking your content or methods of distribution.
- **Sharing** – I continuously share updates. Using Hootsuite and SocialOomph I schedule updates throughout the day, around the clock. Many days have one post per hour. Some days have posts every 15 to 30 minutes. Since Twitter moves pretty fast, it's not a big deal to most users. I link to posts on my blog from time to time, but those posts do not make up the majority of my Tweets. Australia's No. 1 Social Media Guru Jeff Bullas, whom I met at a conference we both spoke at in Mumbai, India, got me started on using SocialOomph. It's similar

to Hootsuite, but allows me to set a recurrence interval schedule for updates. They continue repeating. I was doing some of that manually on Hootsuite.

- **Responding** – When people talk to me on Twitter, I respond. Now, sometimes – not that often, really – people try to keep an unnecessary argument going. In those cases, I just stop the discussion or tell them that "I have nothing else to add." I try to have meaningful conversations with people.
- **Retweeting** – I retweet people's updates when it fits with the topics I normally tweet about and if it's interesting.
- **Offline** – Share your Twitter handle with people offline. For example, when I speak at conferences, every single slide I show has my Twitter handle on it. Depending on the conference, I might also wear a T-shirt with my Twitter handle on it.

There are other ways to build your audience. You can, for example, use promoted posts (basically ads on Twitter) to reach a larger audience.

Growing audiences or communities – depending on your perspective – takes time, but it's possible to do it in an authentic and meaningful way for your brand and your audience.

Stories spread when others share them

All the potential great things that we do are for naught if nobody shares our content.

A brand's social media engagement takes off when others do the sharing. When others share our stories on social media, it's an added endorsement. These people don't have to share what we've created, but when they do, people in their social networks pay attention.

I'm chatty on social media. So are the brands I've worked with, and it helps them digitally brand themselves. But the best results come when **others** share on social media what the brand created.

I've seen this happen in a number of projects now.
I ran a blog called Kids and Tech to share some of my then 6-year-old's comments and musings about technology, media consumption and related topics.

The blog was well-received, and my daughter enjoyed helping me post updates. We published a post on Valentine's Day 2014 that discussed how we ordered flowers for Mom. Shortly after publishing, it was shared and liked by a number of people, which led to it jumping up to become the site's most-read post. When others share to social media what we produce, it will spread much quicker. Granted, some people can get posts to be quite successful on their own when they have huge followings.

Social media: Where discussion happens

A few years ago, I set up a site that displayed videos of speakers pitching ideas at a community event. People could comment on the videos and share them. There was hardly any discussion on the website, but many of the videos had dozens of shares to social media networks. A lot of discussion and commenting happened there instead.

People were really engaged. Discussion happened, but not always in the place where it was easy for me to measure and track. Keep in mind, I couldn't see some discussions due to a person's privacy settings on those social networks.

In another example, in 2012, I helped develop and publish the Cedar Rapids RAGBRAI site and related social media accounts. RAGBRAI is an annual bike ride across Iowa in which 10,000 riders make overnight stops in cities, crisscrossing the state west to east. In 2012, Cedar Rapids was an overnight stop.

The RAGBRAI site again showed the power of social media. We had just kicked off our theme contest – asking the public to submit a tagline for the Cedar Rapids RAGBRAI stop on July 26, 2012. Local TV and newspapers encouraged people to submit a suggestion. So did people on Facebook.

We had 180 referrals (where people saw the link to the contest) from Facebook. Twitter was in second place with 22. KWWL.com, one of the local TV stations, was third with 21. The other two TV stations in our market were in the teens.

So why were the Facebook referrals so high? For one, Facebook has critical mass. It is the most-used social network in Iowa and elsewhere. Plus, many people shared the link through their networks, and then their friends continued sharing the link with their networks. It spread. Facebook makes sharing easy and people rallied around the movement.

Social media continues to be a great way to connect with people, add value to our communities and even build a business. We want to share our own content. Audiences expect it. But it won't spread until others start sharing it.

It's important to participate. Now! The questions of when to join a trend or launch a product on social media strategy are top-of-mind for many organizations today. Some even wonder if they can out-wait a trend. Maybe things will go back to the good old' days.

Does anyone really believe that? I don't. Where those days even that good?

Think about Facebook and Twitter – the more established networks. They aren't new, but many organizations continue to evaluate what they should do on them – if anything at all. Some attempts aren't that social at all and mistake the networks as advertisement delivery channels.

The brands that are using them correctly and effectively – for the most part – hopped on the bandwagon years ago. They experimented. They may not have been the first, but they were among the early adopters. Early adopters have head starts. Start now and adjust as you go.

Does that mean organizations shouldn't hop on a network now? Is it too late? Nope, it's not. Starting today is better than not starting at all. A year from today, you can say you have a year under your belt.

The key is to give the strategy some time and not compare your first day to somebody else's 10th year. You know: "Hey, why do they have 500,000 followers and I only have 1,000?" Because you just started. Give it time.

It's certainly a fine balance. There are hundreds of social networks that organizations could join, in theory. Many of them are irrelevant to many audiences.

Even MySpace, which I often reference in presentations as not being that relevant to most brands I work with, still sees 59 million monthly visitors. It's pretty much become an entertainment and musician site. So if that's your niche, you probably should pay attention. If it's not, don't go there. I know I don't.

Sometimes it's about getting involved quickly to see if the involvement might be worth it. In addition, being first in a particular field or industry can lead to earned media. Those newspaper articles or a TV news story can raise awareness for your organization.

I remember the firsts for social media networks on media channels: "So-and-so set up the donation drive entirely through Facebook."

That was only news the first time it happened, because it was new. The second organization doing the exact same thing – especially in the same media market – wouldn't get the same kind of coverage. Old news!

So there are pros and cons of being an early adopter. In general, I think it's OK to hop on the bandwagon early, but first consider these points:

- Is our target audience/community active on the network?

- Would we fit in? If yes, how?
- What would we say to add to the experience?
- Who will post to the network, monitor conversations and respond (a.k.a. workflow)?
- How will we measure success?

Don't be afraid to get involved and try, but make an educated decision. Quickly. Don't let the planning take so long that you need a new plan by the time you are ready to start because things have changed so much. The only way to see movement is by participation.

Usually, what I've seen is that when we share blog content on an ongoing basis (at least once a week) and make sure it's relevant, unique and maybe even occasionally inspiring, traffic – or engagement – will go up. Slowly. A little bit more every month.

Additionally, distributing and reformatting content for different social media networks helps with engagement on those networks and on the blog. More and more people will read your content, engage with you there and, at some point, even click over (and maybe subscribe) to your blog.

Why I (may) retweet competitors

With all that talk surrounding competitors, let's talk about sharing competitors' or potential competitors' content. I do it from time to time. Sometimes unknowingly.

Why would I ever acknowledge competitors and – even worse, perhaps – why would I retweet (on Twitter) and share their message for them?

There are some people and organizations I would never retweet. No matter what they say, I don't want to be associated with them. Period.

Sometimes, though, potential competitors share something worth re-sharing. If I think my followers would enjoy it, I likely will re-share it.

Why? They might steal business from you, some would say. That might happen, but it's unlikely that one Tweet will kill my opportunities and enhance theirs so dramatically that I have no more projects to work on. I'm usually complaining how every day could use, like, six more hours anyway.

For the purpose of this chapter, I checked how many times on average I tweet. In one recent 28-day period in 2015, I averaged almost 100 Tweets daily. One hundred!

Many of my social media posts are original content, pulled from my Authentic Storytelling Project posts or things I've thought of while walking, traveling or doing some other, unrelated activity. I share other people's posts from time to time, though I didn't see an easy way to count those retweets.

So retweeting somebody else is just one of many updates. And Twitter moves fast, so chances are people see retweets as part of my overall collection of Tweets anyway.

And just because we ignore the competition doesn't make it go away.

I usually find it easier to retweet without links. Even though many Twitter users do not click on links, there's always the chance they will click on the link that I just shared. It's much easier to agree with and amplify a short Tweet than a longer article that might get changed or have some interesting call to action attached to it. I'm much more selective when it comes to retweeting links to articles.

The bottom-line question I ask myself before I retweet is this: Do the people who are connected with me care about this? If they do, I might retweet it. If I think they don't and if it can reflect negatively on me, I likely will not.

Include hyperlinks when relevant

Hyperlinks in blog posts go along the same line. They can from time to time link to competitors, and all external hyperlinks link to other websites, obviously. Ha.

I read online articles that refer to other sites and sources but don't link to them. Sometimes they spell out the other domain name but don't link to it through a hyperlink. What's the reader to do? Copy and paste the text into their browser to check out the site?

It's even less user-friendly when links are spelled out like this: authenticstorytelling(dot)net. Not only do web users have to copy and paste, they also have to delete and add characters to navigate to the site. While that might seem like a minor inconvenience, it is an inconvenience. Why not just add the link?

I believe the best link strategies include outbound hyperlinks.

It's often an unfortunate attempt to hold on to audience. Don't leave our site. I repeat! Do not leave our site. We have you, and we aren't letting you go. We know that you can leave very easily, no matter what. We just won't admit that.

That said, sometimes when links are added, they don't work. I would suggest that after adding a hyperlink, test the link. For example, I test every link after publishing a post, just to make sure it's going where it's supposed to go.

Advantages of including links

Some publishers might have good reasons not to link to a specific site. For example, when an article is about a harmful, malicious site, I wouldn't link to it.

In general, though, relevant hyperlinks add value to our readers:

- Links make the web great and connect us to more information.
- Others might become aware of your site after you link to them. I review referral traffic regularly and visit new sites that link to me.

Best practices for link strategies

Link through a hyperlink to other external (and internal) content when:

- You are quoting the content.
- It adds additional value to your readers.
- You are commenting on the content.

Opinions differ on whether you should have an outbound link open in a new window or in the same window. With the growth in mobile traffic, I favor allowing the link to open in the same window. Opening new windows – especially on mobile devices – might be seen as an inconvenience by users. There's lots of disagreement on this, though.

In a nutshell, linking when it's relevant can help your content, reputation and business.

We love to hide behind disclaimers ...

As we are sharing our own and other people's stories on social media, there are certain dangers associated with public participation. What if a story backfires? What if we say the "wrong thing?" Sometimes people and organizations think disclaimers are the answer. I've seen versions of these:

- All Tweets are my own.
- Tweets do not represent my employer's view.
- RTs (retweets) are not endorsements.
- Following somebody isn't an endorsement.

I've even seen some people link to additional pages of disclaimers. I'm sure those will be read as often as those "Terms and Conditions" many of us accept in a second-and-a-half when installing a new app on our phones or computers.

So do all these disclaimers mean or do anything? Well, they cover us when we say something that our boss, or whoever, doesn't like. Maybe. It's debate-able.

Ultimately, disclaimers can't prevent offline consequences for online behaviors, and most people reading updates likely don't even remember them. Plus, they take up valuable space to share more relevant information about yourself and what you are talking about on a social media network.

Personally, I usually don't include any disclaimers in my bios. I did add a tongue-in-cheek one on Twitter before: Most Tweets are no opinion. They are fact. Ha.

I've learned that people aren't differentiating between unique and curated content in a stream. At one time, people offline continued saying to me that they "love the stuff I write online." I wasn't blogging much then and was mostly sharing other people's stories. People took other people's stories as *my* stories – despite me never saying that they were or even saying that I agreed.

Disclaimers might be needed from a legal perspective. Maybe. And there are things that some people believe cannot be revealed publicly – like trade secrets, for example.

But if nobody reads disclaimers or believes them, what's the point? Are they helping authentic discussions? I would argue that they don't.

Let's pick on this disclaimer: "Tweets are my own, not my employer's."

What does that allow me to do?

- Rip on a business partner? I wouldn't advise that.
- Rip on the company or co-workers? That wouldn't help morale, now, would it?
- Share a negative story? People can do that even without a disclaimer. Just be aware of the consequences.

It's always interesting when CEOs put this disclaimer on their profiles because I'm sure people reading along will totally see the CEO as unaffiliated with his or her company. Right.

This reminds me of a sheriff with whom I worked a few years ago. Sheriffs in Iowa are elected law enforcement officers. He said to me:

"I campaign while on the job."

"Really? Is that allowed?"

"I'm always on the job – even during off hours. Plus, people see me as the sheriff even when I'm out for dinner."

Bingo.

The line between you and your organization is hard to draw. The higher up you are in an organization, the harder it will be for the public to believe there's a difference between the off-duty and on-duty CEO.

And what does it mean to say something wrong anyway? Something is factually wrong? OK, that can be corrected.

Or maybe it's something that the powers-that-be disagree with. That's an entirely different discussion. What's wrong with allowing different opinions? This is the Participation Age after all.

Or perhaps what was shared is just offensive. This can happen when people try to be funny. Funny writing is hard. Funny writing that aligns with somebody's professional position is even harder.

What's better than disclaimers? How about judgment? Have a discussion with folks about their use of social media, and help them use it in the most meaningful way to them, their company and their community. And that doesn't mean everything has to be positive all the time. And intent matters. Ask the people in prison for it.

Seriously, intent matters in the stories and information that we share on our blogs and social media channels.

What was our intent when we posted what we posted?

Did we try to teach? Did we try to show off to somebody? Did we (knowingly) spread incorrect information? Did we try to be politically incorrect?

Why did we do it? The intent matters.

Sometimes we might misinterpret somebody's intent or something was taken out of context. When somebody quotes us correctly, but we say, "That was taken out of context," do we really mean, "It wasn't my intent to come across like that"? Maybe. Being taken out of context comes back to intent. Did they intend to be misleading with that quote, or did they actually think it was fair and accurate?

Yes, I know that the actual words were spoken, but the additional words spoken around them don't make much sense or have a different meaning. The intent can come back to our relationship with the person asking the questions, and even their body language, which can be hard to read when the query is sent through a Tweet.

Maybe, just maybe, the person picked less-than-perfect words by mistake. So, instead of a having a digital lynch mob jump on him or her, what if we ask a clarification question first: I read your post this way. Is that right? Can you explain that further?

Certainly some statements people make are better kept in one's head. So maybe they actually intended them exactly the way they said them. Maybe they just weren't prepared for the digital onslaught of opinions. Once we share something publicly, be prepared for people to respond publicly.

Can we change our intent after the digital lynch mob has gotten hold of us? Probably not. Sometimes people say after the fact that they didn't intend to cause that reaction, but does that mean they still meant what they said?

Intent matters. Let's make it count for something. I try to share with good intentions – even when I know it may ruffle somebody's feathers.

Of course, intent only matters when we actually share stories publicly. **It's actually quite simple** to get started.

There's one piece that is vital to the authentic storytelling process. Once you made up your mind to participate, the No. 1 way to get started is to recognize the stories that happen in front of us, react and then actually share them!

It sounds so simple but is actually harder than it sounds. Sometimes we focus on strategy (which is super important).

Other times, we focus on the tools: Here's a blog. It's set up...

"Please blog now."

"About what?"

Exactly.

Let's talk about tools for a moment – especially since this section focuses on social media – which basically is a tool. Some of my talks in the later part of 2015 have been about tools:

- At WordCamp Omaha, a WordPress conference, I talked about the wonderful Jetpack plugin and how it makes content distribution so much easier.
- At SUGCON North America, a Sitecore conference in New Orleans, my talk focused on when to pick Sitecore for your blogging project and when to go with WordPress.

I love WordPress, and my site runs on WordPress. I also love the Jetpack plugin, which has been created by Automattic – the makers of WordPress – and combines a number of popular plugins into one install. It helps me focus on content creation instead of shopping for plugins. Sitecore is also a great tool, as I mentioned in my SUGCON talk. But people use them for different purposes.

Sitecore's biggest advantage is personalization. In a nutshell, Sitecore can deliver truly personalized content to people. Based on my interests, it would serve different content to me than it does to you. It's personalized based on our needs and interests. In theory, that will eliminate all useless content to you – the end consumer!

But, here's the thing these tools – as great and useful as they might be – won't do for you:

They will not help you spot the stories worth sharing, produce them and share them. You still have to do that on your own.

In an organization, you need to have a culture that encourages storytelling – one where employees keep an eye out for things worth sharing and that are then actually shared. Yes, publicly.

The platforms and tools are important pieces to consider. They can make our lives harder or much easier depending on the ease of use.

The same is true with content gathering tools. It used to be that you'd have to sit in front of a desktop computer to write posts and get a professional photographer to take photos or buy a stock image. Today, all of those things can be done from our smartphones. Yes, there's still a time and a place for professional photography, and for sitting down and writing a longer piece from a desktop computer (which is more likely a laptop), but many stories can be created from just the smartphone.

I mention this here because I sense a trend that some people focus too much on the tools and not as much on what to actually use those tools for.

The example I give is this unfortunately common blog example:

- Somebody launches a blog.
- They publish a blog post saying that they will blog weekly about XYZ.
- Then nothing for six months.
- They publish a blog post that says: "Sorry, I haven't published anything for six months. I will start now."

But their blog looked really nice and was well designed! These people certainly had tools to publish content at their disposal, but they didn't. The right tool didn't help them continuously publish content.

The right tools are important and make our lives easier, but we still have to figure out what we are going to talk about! No tool – at least not currently – can do that for us.

Use the tools, but focus on the relevancy of the stories around us. Stories surround us. Some are worth sharing. Some are routine and don't warrant much publicity.

Some fantastic stories, though, can be wrongfully categorized as routine, and sometimes we don't even categorize or spot stories at all. We just move on with our daily routines. Task done. Check. Move on to the next thing. Catching stories is the farthest thing from our minds.

Interestingly, missing stories worth sharing even happens to professional storytellers like content marketers or journalists. I remember times when a handful of journalists had access to the same event and people and even were near each other. All came back with and shared completely different stories.

One person even got a story that some editors thought was worth re-reporting for the competing newspaper.

"How did our reporter miss this?" they wondered.

It's so easy in theory to catch and tell stories. It's much harder in practice. The trick is to spot stories when they happen and then react. Even when we try, we can miss them.

So how do you get there?

- Encourage people to share stories.
- Call out the great ones. Recognize people for them and for sharing them!
- Be involved. It's much easier to share the stories of which we are a part.

All the tools, tips and tricks to share stories don't do us any good if we don't spot the ones worth sharing in the first place.

Once you spot stories, you have to find a way to publish them. I certainly have started writing blog posts that I didn't finish and trashed for one reason or another. That's OK from time to time, but don't make it a habit.

Some common ones:

1. My point wasn't clear even to me. Ha.
2. It wasn't that engaging of a story.
3. Too many political waters to swim through once it publishes.

Point No. 3 above is probably the easiest to use to not publish something. There certainly are situations when it applies, but just because an actual authentic story is potentially *politically* incorrect doesn't mean that it's *actually* incorrect. Of course, not every battle is worth picking, either.

The trashed or unpublished words on my blog are in the minority – by far. Something to consider as your content marketing and storytelling strategy kicks off: **Make sure to find a way to publish the stories that are happening.**

Formatting vs. storytelling

Sometimes instead of focusing on telling good stories, we focus on processes or formatting issues. Don't get me wrong here, posts should look a certain way (great!), but if we have nothing to format, it doesn't make any difference that we know how to format it. I see posts like this all the time – probably weekly, if not more often:

- How to correctly format your blog post
- Eight things every blog post needs to include
- Five new tools to help you blog
- Our 12-step process to get your blog post done

Some of this information is useful and when applied properly can help us improve our blogging and storytelling.

But these kind of posts also can serve as enablers for procrastination. When we focus too much on some things, we focus less on other things.

I once read that Steve Jobs wore the same type of outfit every day because not having to make a decision on dress ("does this match?" which is a question I wrestle with most days) frees up brain power to think about other things – like inventing the iPhone.

The same is true with authentic storytelling and content marketing, especially when we first get started.

We can spend all the time we have on formatting posts, debating why a story should or shouldn't be published and even lengths of posts. The bottom line is that process – great ways to measure or format – won't make much of a difference if we don't share meaningful stories that are unique to us. If we have nothing of value to share, it won't make a difference that it looks pretty.

My suggestion – and I follow this myself – would be to first focus on finding relevant, interesting stories. Of course, make sure they have something to do with your business goals, but focus on finding those rock star stories. Stories that are meaningful to the audience will outperform stories that are formatted nicely but have little substance behind them.

Keep in mind that in a perfect world, we publish stories that are meaningful and follow some of those best practices of appearance. We should strive for that. Absolutely.

7 tips to increase your blog traffic by 72.4 percent in 33 days

Formatting posts are often list posts. While I don't love formatting tips posts, I do love list posts. They set a clear expectation of how much information I can expect.

They often are easy to read – I mean scan. I can start reading each item and decide if I need to keep reading each explanation. I'm in charge of my time. List posts perform well – which is why so many bloggers do them.

But here's where I run into problems with web headlines like the one on this chapter. I doubt very much that a 72.4 percent increase can be replicated. Even if every exact step is followed.

First of all, that's a super precise promise.

Second, things change. Social media networks change. How many people see a post changes. Think Facebook reach and how that has changed to a model where you can pretty much only reach people when you pay for it. User behavior changes. Who knows what else changes by the time somebody reads our post?

One day I can promote a Tweet for $50 and get one number of click-throughs and impressions. The next day, I do the same thing and get a totally different result. I did nothing different. Something changed somewhere.

And something is always changing. Take a look at technology news headlines. Some changes are minor, and we wouldn't have even noticed them without the article. Some changes are major, and we notice because we don't like them. Some changes are actually helpful.

Telling readers X number of steps will yield a Y increase is easy to comprehend. Some consumers might even believe they can duplicate the results.

In the headline I used for this section, adding the time element makes it appear that the same result can be accomplished fairly quickly. In reality, content marketing and blogging projects take time and are long-term investments.

Some results certainly can be duplicated, and we can always learn from each other. But our articles need to keep the promise of their headlines. When they don't, trust erodes. Sometimes trust goes out the window because a headline overpromises.

We all have a choice with the content we share. We can decide which movement to join:

1) Write the most clicked-on headlines whether they are accurate or not.

OR

2) Write headlines and content that is authentic and tells a great and engaging story without overpromising.

Authentic storytellers – in content marketing and elsewhere – tell the best stories that add long-term value. Their stories get read and shared and are helpful because they are authentic. You can decide in seconds which movement you'll join. The implementation will take a bit longer.

Really, overstating things will usually just lead to one thing: Audiences tuning out. Here's another example:

Consider this letter I received in the mail. The outside of the envelope says: OPEN IMMEDIATELY: IMPORTANT INFORMATION REGARDING YOUR TELEVISION ACCOUNT.

I had cut satellite television from our list of bills, so this could be important, I thought. Something might be going on with the bill. Maybe the company didn't get the equipment we mailed back. Who knows?

Nope, none of those were the case. The envelope was stuffed with ads and offers to come back because the company "missed us," which of course meant they missed our money. A bit of an overstatement on the envelope.

Other more authentic messages for that envelope could have been:

- Special "please come back" deal enclosed.
- We want you back. Special offer enclosed.

- Do you miss your sports channels? You can come back anytime. We won't hold it against you!

I've mentioned many times that attention from the consumer can be hard to come by. People are showered with thousands of messages a day. Yes, we need to stand out to even get people's attention. But attention gained through overstated or misleading headlines won't help us sustain that attention. We get a one-time look – if that – and people move on.

I prefer to do business with companies that use authentic and completely accurate wording in their communications. It's part of authentic storytelling – or, in this case, authentic marketing.

Put your content on many channels

With that, we want to keep all channels in mind and remember that they interact together. Multi-channel content strategy is a concept where the content creator keeps all relevant distribution channels in mind.

Around 2010, some communicators and marketers advocated that every platform (email newsletter, Twitter, website, etc.) needs unique and original content.

Multi-channel content strategy communicators still believe that every channel should be used to connect with people, but channels don't need completely original content from an organization, business or person.

Consider this Tweet from December 23, 2013: Writing a book and then pulling 1,000 or so Tweets out of it is an example of multi-channel #contentstrategy. @Ctrappe.

That Tweet is an example of multi-channel content strategy. Instead of just sending out links to the book's Amazon listing, the author might pull out short tidbits and use them as Tweets. Or related topics can be used as short blog posts. In fact, this book followed the blog-to-book strategy. Most everything in here was previously published on my blog, The Authentic Storytelling Project.

This multi-channel content strategy is possible for many stories. For example, many Tweets can be turned into longer blog posts, and versions of that same blog post could be turned into a newspaper guest column. Depending on your organizational goals and budgets, the same content can be turned into a printed brochure that you hand out at the office.

Your audiences – for the most part – won't know (or even care) that it's all the same content, just reformatted. Even if they knew, content is so plentiful and people move from one thing to another so fast these days that most people won't mind. In fact, seeing closely related headlines more than once can encourage people to engage with content on the second or subsequent touch.

Respond quickly

I've talked a lot about content creation and distribution, but responding quickly might be nearly as important as what we actually say, as Scott Stratton said during his keynote at Content Marketing World in Cleveland in September 2014.

I believe that's true. If I post something to social media – a question to a brand, for example – I expect to get an answer now. Right now. Hello?

A study published by Forbes in 2014 said that most users expect a response within an hour. Got it. You'll have to be speedy. But speedy, meaningless responses are just that – meaningless.

Reponses falling into this category are "canned ones" that could be used in response to any number of social media posts. Adding the person's name to a canned response doesn't make it any better. We've all heard canned responses, and most of us hate hearing them when we have a problem.

Examples include:

- "We are sorry to hear that."
- "Thank you for stopping in."
- "Sorry you are having problems."
- "Thank you for your patience."

Who said I'm patient? Better responses are those that specifically respond to the person's questions, solve his or her problem and are unique.

We likely won't share a generic Tweet that some brand sent us. But we might share a unique and interesting story like this:

During the 2012 Olympics, the NBC Olympics Twitter account tweeted a fact about beach volleyball. I asked a question. The NBC Olympics account didn't reply, but April Ross, one of the players, did. It was great to see somebody using social media this way. Here's the exchange:

I've been sharing this story for years now. She is perhaps the only volleyball player whose name I actually recall.

Would I become her advocate and share when she's in a match on TV? Probably. Would I cheer for her? Yup.

Would I do those things if that interaction hadn't happened? Maybe. But now it's different. It was a small but memorable experience.

Let's talk about airlines. They get picked on frequently on social media, but they respond and actually try to help. It's actually easier to get things done with them on social media than calling them.

Operating the different customer service channels in silos is likely the easiest, and that's why a lot of companies are following that model:

- Social media people answer on social media
- Phone people answer on the phones

There may be some crossover here and there, but in my experience it seems that the social media people with problems they can't or aren't supposed to help with tell you to call the phone people, who then put you on hold. Now, there are some things that can be resolved on social media and that's great, but there are still plenty of situations where it's much easier to talk to each other live and not through the written word.

But British Airways does a nice job moving between channels to help customers. Here's an example:

In November 2015, I was booked on British Airways on a trip to Mumbai to speak at a blogging conference. I tried to change my seat online without luck, so I tweeted at British Airways for help. It's what you do in 2015.

Now, sometimes people tell me that customer service is better when you have an established relationship or are a high-valued customer to a company. That certainly might be true in cases, but up to this point I had never flown British Airways and was only booked through them because that's who partners with American Airlines, my main airline, for London-Mumbai flights.

Anyway, I couldn't get it to work and direct messaged British Airways my cell number on Twitter. They promptly called to get the information they needed to help. Everything was resolved, and I wasn't once placed on hold or asked by some automated voice to spell what they couldn't understand. Great service across channels.

You cannot have a lengthy approval process

To accomplish this kind of feat – even across just one channel – you cannot have lengthy approval processes or lame scripts. The difficulty when speed and relevancy are expected comes from some old-school organizations that want to approve all corporate communications.

Good luck crafting a perfect marketing message response that works for all problems and questions. Remember, as soon as you send that "masterfully crafted" message, one person or another most likely will immediately ask another question. And then what?

The keys to communicating in this fast-moving digital world for organizations, brands and other people are:

- Embrace transparency and participation.
- Know what you stand for! You can't please everyone.
- Have a point person (or team for larger organizations) who has the knowledge and authority to respond now.

Do not reply to this email! (Sigh)

One of the great signs of organizations not being ready for two-way communications are those Do Not Reply emails. The Do Not Reply sender's name is not very inviting. It does not build relationships. It screams at me that the sender doesn't want to talk to me.

I get that there can be financial advantages to not allowing people to reply. Because if it's allowed, they might, and it won't help organizations when they do not monitor and respond to replies. Clearly, to have somebody monitor and reply in a meaningful way costs money.

Unfortunately, the unanswered email (or Tweet) is all too common.

In essence Do Not Reply emails say:

- Here's an email from us.
- Don't dare respond to it.

Sounds like one-way communication to me. Here's our message. Take it or leave it.

Some trendsetters actually encourage people to reply. I've seen notes like this:

> *Yes, this is an automated mass email, but we are happy to hear from you. Simply reply with your questions and comments. We will take them to heart and respond when necessary.*

And consumers do respond. It builds a relationship with the brand. It's about communication and being heard. And, of course, since many organizations aren't responding to emails, Tweets or contact forms from websites, responding to people can help brands stand out. It can be a differentiator.

Video, pictures and more are great tools in addition to writing

Live streaming might help us be more authentic publicly

With the resurgence of live streaming tools in 2015, live broadcasting is back in the headlines. These live streaming tools might help us be more comfortable with our stories, look like humans on video and behave like people do.

Of course, live streams on the Internet are nothing new. When I worked for a regional media company a few years ago, we routinely streamed events online. Since then, Google Hangouts have made live video chats another public option. In theory, people could do a Hangout and broadcast an event that way, too.

Then two new livestreaming apps entered the market in 2015: Meerkat launched first, and Periscope, which is owned by Twitter, launched a few weeks later. People can live stream whatever is in front of them from their smartphones with these new apps. Both basically do the same thing with a few variations.

You simply install the respective apps on your smartphone, connect to your Twitter account, enable the microphone and camera, point and go live. The stream will be shared in the app, and a link will be shared on your Twitter stream. It's the beauty of these new apps: It's so easy.

Live streaming can be an easy-to-use tool for anyone – people and organizations alike – to share their authentic stories. Keep in mind that once a live stream is live, it's live, and people can see and hear whatever is being broadcast. Live streams can't be edited while live, so whatever is happening or is being said is really sharing the actual story.

That might not be as exciting as it sounds. I saw people live stream their dog walks (I got bored walking my own dog when I had one!) and drinking a smoothie. For testing purposes, I live streamed my eight-month-old sitting in the living room. Her stream even got 12 viewers and a bunch of likes – called hearts on Periscope.

One girl was having a conversation with a few dozen viewers and stopped for a moment to feed her dog while live on the air. It actually reminded us that she's human. That's what humans do. Their dog needs food, so they feed it.

Certainly, there's room for improvement for people to broadcast more than the mundane. The guy walking his dogs, for example, was commenting on which dog was going, or not going, to the bathroom. TMI. And I'm even a dog person.

Many authentic stories are perhaps a tad boring. That likely means they won't keep people's attention in the long term. But there are meaningful ways to use these tools.

Some things that might be worth broadcasting:

- Presentations, for the people who can't attend in person.
- Breaking news events. I'm thinking of the time I was stuck at Chicago O'Hare International Airport after a fire. That could have been worth live streaming – but only to an extent. I wasn't even near the fire, which was miles away. But I was near a lot of people who were stuck until who knew when.

- Visually appealing scenes. One person was showing a swimming pool in a warmer location. That was kind of cool, but really, it's not video and could have been a tweeted photo.
- Events. Organizations could live stream dedications, award ceremonies and so on.

The trick in live streaming – as in much authentic storytelling – is spotting the stories, the opportunities, as they are about to happen, and then starting to go live. Our audiences (I hope) will get to see an engaging and relevant live-streamed story. A lot of people just have conversations on Periscope. Think selfie-video – they just talk about whatever comes to mind. Depending on what they talk about and what their points are, this can be super interesting – or super boring.

'Talking heads' are not usually good video

In general, though, "talking heads" videos are not that engaging.

We see the studies: Video drives engagement. So let's all produce more videos. But just because something is shot with a video camera doesn't make it great video.

There are exceptions, but some "videos" that are not that great include:

- Talking heads. Make it a podcast!
- Picture after picture. That's just a slideshow.
- Reading a script. Just email it to me, and I'll read it later.

You can likely think of other examples. But I think we can agree the best video tells a story and takes advantage of video's ability to show movement. That's why real-life videos of people doing less-than-smart things are so powerful or why videos of violence (sometimes involving police officers) are so eye-opening and widely viewed. They tell the story in a way a picture or words couldn't.

Videos are best used when the story demands it. Our communities (a.k.a. audiences) will thank us for using the best tools to share our stories most effectively. Sometimes that will be video. Other times it will be something else.

Use video when it's the best tool to share the story – not because you want to do video.

The exception for talking head videos might be on Periscope. All kinds of people have a conversation with dozens or hundreds of other people. They talk to their phones and technically it's just a talking head. But those talking head videos are different because they are interactive. The Scoper, which is what Periscope broadcasters are called, is talking, but also responding to people's comments typed on the screen. It's much closer to a conversation than a produced video.

There certainly are YouTube stars who have quite a following for their talking head videos, but they have some specific personality, typically aren't just reading a prompter and are the exception.

Video interviews help us tell stories

Video is a great tool to gather stories. Recording interviews of people opens up options for sharing their stories aside from the written word. Of course, we should shoot more video so we don't end up with just talking heads.

Even if you've haven't shot video before, cameras continue to get easier and easier to use. Small devices shoot great quality video today. Adding a microphone to the mix makes the recording of interviews in a quality format that audiences will want to watch affordable to many of us.

You can record an entire interview and then use bits and pieces of it in different capacities. Let's take a look at the pros, cons and equipment.

Before video interviews

When I first worked as a print journalist in the early 2000s, I would interview people and tell their stories daily. I would take handwritten notes that I would later use to quote people. Yes, I really believed that I got quotes written down word for word.

But, as you can imagine, this kind of interviewing can be challenging. It's not impossible, but there's a chance you might miss an answer. Recording interviews offers a number of advantages.

Video interviews: The positives

Recording our interviews allows us to:

- Focus on the conversation during the interview without trying to get the right words written down.

- Use audio (or video) clips of the interview later on the website/social media.
- You can play back the video to review what somebody said. It makes misquotes less likely, but keep in mind that people can misspeak from time to time.

Video interviews: The drawbacks

There are some disadvantages to recording interviews on video:

- People might not want to be recorded. I usually try to explain the advantages and, if they still don't want to be recorded, we'll just talk. A good story can be gathered and told many different ways.
- It takes some time to set up the camera equipment, hook the microphone on the person and do a mic check.
- You have to watch the footage again to get the quotes and soundbites. But really, you'd have to find the quotes if you were taking pages upon pages of notes, too.
- Technology doesn't always work. Make sure the battery doesn't run out while you are recording. Take an extra battery, just in case. Remember to push record, take the lens cap off, etc.

Video equipment

You have plenty of options for equipment to record video interviews and to shoot B-roll video. You can buy reasonably good equipment for under $1,500. I've even seen people shoot decent video – with decent audio – with a smartphone. So that could be an option for you.

If you prefer a camera with more features, the Canon VIXIA HF M41 Full HD Camcorder might be a suitable option. I've used it for a few years and have had few – all minor – problems. I love the compactness and quality of footage. At the time of writing this, it was selling for around $1,000.

Bad audio can kill an otherwise great story. Using a good microphone is important. The Audio Technica ATR288W VHF Battery-Powered TwinMic Microphone System works well with the Canon camera mentioned above and provides good audio. Make sure to have extra batteries while on a shoot.

You'll find many advantages to recording interviews on video. They can help us get accurate quotes and soundbites, help us engage more during an interview and allow us to easily distribute the story across several channels.

Having the best equipment for a specific situation, knowing how to use it, and using it with the different channels of distribution in mind, can help us tell better authentic stories.

7 tips to shoot good video

Everyone can do video. Many of us carry phones with cameras. Most of those phones even shoot high-definition video. But just because we have some of the tools, that doesn't mean we can use them perfectly.

Some of us – including me – have learned this the hard way. The key is to learn from missteps and from others. I've learned much of what I know when it comes to smartphone video storytelling by trial and error. Remember, everything you publish is a reflection on you and the organizations with which you associate.

Here are my top tips to keep in mind when using your smartphone to shoot video:

1) Get good audio.

Not having good audio can make or break a video. Your options:

- Buy a lavalier microphone you can clip on the person you are interviewing.
- Be close enough that your phone's internal mic will work. (This may feel too close to your interview subject, but it's doable.)
- Use a second smartphone to shoot the audio and then later sync the audio and video. Keep in mind that this takes more time than just shooting it all on one device, but it can improve the video's quality.

2) Hold shots longer than you think is necessary.

It's easy to see something worth shooting, point the camera, think that you've got it and stop recording. Once you play the footage back, chances are the shot is shorter than you thought. So always shoot longer than it feels like you should. Slowly count to five or ten and then stop shooting.

3) Move to zoom.

Don't use your camera's zoom function. If you need to get a closer shot, use your feet to zoom and move closer to the subject. This will help with video quality.

4) Tell a story.

Before you start shooting, think about the story you want to tell.

5) Hold the camera steady.

You don't want your audience to get seasick. Hold the shot. Don't move quickly. Not talking to others around you (other than the interviewee) also helps.

6) Hold the camera correctly.

Some phones will adjust the final video's orientation, but some phones make this harder. So make sure you are holding the phone in the way that will upload the video correctly – and not upside down, for example. Most phones work best when you hold them horizontally while shooting.

7) Test everything before shooting your video.

Make sure you have enough storage on your phone, that the mic works and that you know how to upload the video to the Internet. This could be through YouTube or WordPress apps, for example. The key is to test the workflow.

Shooting video has become easier, and great stories can be told through simple videos.

For pictures: Move to find the best angle

Since we are talking about multimedia, let's talk about some simple steps to get decent photos. I'm a big advocate of blog posts having unique and original photos with them – even when the photos are not award-winning. Keep taking photos and chances are that one will work with a new blog post. It's better than unrelated stock art that everyone can buy.

Since we relate to people, it's important to use good photos of real people with our authentic stories. Anyone can buy stock images. Take real photos. Even if it's just with your iPhone.

I was reminded of the importance of moving for better angle when I used my iPhone to take some photos of my two girls in the colorful fall leaves we have here in the Midwest. I really only needed/wanted one picture, but I had to move a couple of times to end up with my favorite shot, which is this one:

But this wasn't the first picture I took. The girls were facing the other way when we started, looking into the setting sun. The first shot looked like this:

It only took us four pictures to figure out that this wasn't going to work. So they turned the other way, and I moved to the other side of them. Still on my knees, the next pose looked like this:

Better, but who wants to see a sidewalk in the background, and the light was kind of strange. After a few more snaps, I realized I might have a good shot if I stood up. As I was standing up, everyone, including the baby, instinctively looked up at me, and I ended up with a great picture. I later cropped it and added a filter, which led to the picture at the top of this chapter. Much better than where we started.

While the tools available to us and the technological advances continue to make it easier to take pictures, shoot video and create other content, it's still important to not just shoot away but to look for good composition.

Pausing for a moment, asking people to move, taking multiple shots and moving around can get us there.

Think of communications like performances

When we do decide to share our authentic stories through video, pictures, words or really any channel, it's helpful to think of the presentations as performances. It helps us make them more memorable. I speak a lot. Just ask the people who know me. I also have been asked to speak around the globe frequently in recent years.

I enjoy these engagements very much and believe every talk is practice for the next one. I even say that exact thing during some talks – especially when I'm talking about how to effectively share your story in front of groups. Usually, the groups I talk to find this very entertaining. They laugh and, without knowing, just learned something.

People want to be entertained, and they pay much more attention to a great show than me reading slides to them.

I first started realizing this by mistake, of course. I was changing up my presentation style a few years ago to be more rah-rah, fun (yes, jokes) and entertaining.

My goal was to keep people on the edge of their seats. I wanted them to want to be there. Even if they have the option of leaving, they won't. They want to hear what's coming next. They remember what I've said and will even share something about it, maybe at dinner, maybe later. It was memorable and – yes – entertaining.

When I first started performing and stopped giving speeches, somebody gave me a 10 on a 1 to 5 scale and wrote, "So much fun."

And what about the content? I hope it was good, too, but there was no mention of it by this person. That started to be a recurring theme. Fun worked. Of course, authentic storytelling does lend itself to fun. Some topics don't.

The content *must* be good, and I have to present it in a way that is credible. But ultimately, I've found that people remember how I made them *feel.*

You get people to feel something when they react. Positive reactions could be laughter, a thought or a slight disagreement, followed by a moment of a-ha agreement.

Let's talk about a-ha agreements for a moment. This is when you share something that people feel slightly challenged to disagree with. But after a moment, they agree and will remember the mind shift.

One of my favorite examples: I tell the audience that sharing authentic stories is so hard. That's why it's taking a while to get started. OMG, it's so hard.

Many – if not all – nod their heads in agreement. I've even gotten an "Amen" before.

Then I say: And do you know why it's so hard?

*People are edging closer in their seats. * Don't fall off the edge, please!

It's so hard because we say it's so hard. As long as we say that, it won't get any easier. Some people tilt their heads. Others jump to the conclusion of "Oh, yes." Some people vocally agree. I've had audience members turn to their neighbors and loudly say: "THAT is so true. We should stop. It's not hard."

Yes.

Yes.

Yes.

Many – if not all – agree with the total opposite of what we all agreed on 10 seconds earlier. #Boom.

I could have presented that whole thing on one slide – text only, no animations or pictures. But people wouldn't agree, wouldn't learn anything and certainly wouldn't remember it.

We are only memorable when we make people feel something. For me, the trick is to make it all a performance. Yes, I'm still authentic and share only things that, to the best of my knowledge, are true.

But I do work at putting on a show. Don't expect to see me dancing. Or singing. Some of my techniques, however, include:

- Moving around during talks
- Speaking clearly
- Not reading a script
- Changing up my voice
- Looking *at* the audience, not *through* the audience
- Asking the audience questions
- Responding to audience members
- Being unique and being myself (the performance me, not the watching-football-on-a-Sunday me)

Blog posts need to be somewhat entertaining, too. There needs to be some kind of engagement value, which could be entertainment, inspiration and/or education.

Talking to the masses, making it personal

Speeches are different from conversations. Public writing is different from writing a letter to a friend. I remember being taught the differences, and since authority figures teach us things, that means we believe it and live by them. But what if there is no difference and speeches are just like conversations, and public writing (like a blog post) is just like writing a letter to a friend?

Sure, we wouldn't share confidential information, but why are conversations and personal writings more memorable? Because they aren't so formal. They often are fun, too.

"I can't wait to read this formal website with its organizational tone" is something no one said, ever.

On the other hand, when speakers are personable, they are remembered. This is especially important for top leaders, who likely have no time to speak individually to everyone they impact.

So how do you get there? Some thoughts on speaking first:

- Make jokes – they have to be funny to that audience.
- Tell personal stories, but no fluff.
- Talk *to* the audience, not *at* them.
- Ask questions and respond with answers.
- Be aware that you are the entertainment – be entertaining.
- Know that "stiff" is usually not perceived as authentic.
- Reading scrips (without looking up) is also not authentic.

How about writing? The basics apply here, too:

- Tell meaningful stories.
- Write in the first-person
- Do not lecture.
- Get feedback before publishing, but no "editing by committee," which can turn every word into a compromise.

Does storytelling work?

To a degree, the answer depends on what your definition of "work" is. Does true and ongoing authentic storytelling help me get more business? Yes, absolutely. Can I attribute every single conversion to a specific story? Nope. But I can say that my ongoing authentic storytelling projects have brought in customers, retained customers and made an overall impact for myself and clients I've worked with.

Let's dive a bit deeper...

What's the ROI of all this content?

We've heard the questions: What's the ROI (return on investment) for creating all of this content? Shouldn't content marketing be measurable? Every story out the door should bring in $253 per reader.

Some people have tweeted, blogged and Facebooked responses like this:

- What's the ROI of putting on my pants in the morning?
- What's the ROI of being nice?
- What's the ROI of eating lunch?

You get the point, I'm sure. Most of us wouldn't consider leaving the house without pants on. Being nice is not required, but if we aren't, we'll be grumpy and going through the day will probably not be as pleasant as it could be. And we do have to eat lunch – or breakfast or dinner.

Measuring ROI

I love metrics and they often are easy to measure online. Sometimes it can turn into chasing traffic numbers, which is OK to a degree. If we are selling something, we can measure how many people buy something after reading a certain piece of content. We can measure if the red or the green button increases signups to our newsletter. We can track pages per visit, how long people stick around and other behaviors. Those are good and useful things to know, and we should use them to improve the user's experience and help our business. But some important results can't easily be measured.

Measuring a different ROI

Can the ROI only be counted in dollars? Is that the only thing that matters? We want to make money, certainly! But perhaps there's more to content creation than crafting a message we think will make people buy something they may not even have wanted to buy.

Maybe it's about education, community connection and some of those things that aren't nearly as measurable. Maybe it's about sharing authentic stories about our companies, communities and families and documenting them in a way that future generations can look back at them and imagine what our lives were like.

What if the ROI of sharing content comes down to:

- Education.
- Closer connections.

- Self-exploration. For example: Every time I blog, I learn something, even though I'm the one writing it.
- Documentation of history for future generations.
- Creating an organic database surrounding community issues.
- Making actual impressions on each other – not those ad impressions that people ignore.

Maybe the ROI of authentic stories shared by organizations has nothing to do with convincing people to buy something right now. Maybe it's about helping us make sense of our communities and the different parts of it.

Then, after everyone is sharing authentic and meaningful stories, we are more connected, educated and will probably even buy something from each other – if there's something being sold besides knowledge.

Think of it like this: Perhaps, it's about me, you and the stories and conversations that connect us. From time to time, there are also transactions involved, but they don't make up the main piece of our connections.

Measuring story impact is hard

Impressions, click-through rates, "likes" and so on are all social media metrics that help us measure what is and isn't working.

For example, my Tweets had 274,000 impressions in December 2014, a metric that jumped to 455,700 impressions in January 2015. When your reach jumps that much, you notice it.

More people start connecting, retweeting and reaching out for deeper conversations – including partnerships.

I was the guest on two global Twitter chats – one on content marketing and one on storytelling in the workplace. I'm certain that had something to do with the increase.

But with all the metrics at our disposal, social media's true value (a.k.a. return on investment or objective) can be hard to measure at times. Let me illustrate;

If you follow me on Twitter, you know how much I love it. So it was great to see a hashtag sweater picture and comment posted to my Facebook wall by co-worker Angie Toomsen.

Now, I do think that too many hashtags can make Tweets look ugly, but I liked the idea of the hashtag sweater. Plus, I liked that Angie took the time to take and post a picture.

I like to wear T-shirts with messages on them from time to time, so I wondered if I could add a hashtag shirt to my wardrobe. I opened another tab and went to Amazon and started searching for "hashtag T-shirts."

There were a bunch. Many were too silly to wear in public, but I did end up finding one I liked: A #tshirt shirt.

It's clear to see that this purchase can be credited to social media. Angie posted the picture to my Facebook wall, and that's social media. It prompted me to go to Amazon to search for something similar. Without her posting the picture of the gentleman in a hashtag sweater, I would not have made this purchase. I wasn't even thinking about it.

But Facebook won't get credit for the sale. Remember, Angie didn't link to Amazon to let me know that I could buy a similar piece of clothing. I got that idea after seeing her note.

While we can measure a lot of things in the digital world, we can't measure everything, and I would bet that the impact of social media is bigger than we think (and can measure).

And some measurements might be worth less than we think. Gregg Weiss, VP of Social Media at MasterCard, has famously tweeted that just because an impression was served doesn't mean an impression was made. So true. How do you measure that? It's a long-term process for sure.

Many stories are worth sharing

Time has to pass before some stories can be shared

I can tell you that personal stories that connect to people work. Even when they aren't published the second they happened.

In 2014, I wrote the following with two beautiful daughters at home.

My first experience with adding a child to our family was terrible. In 2006, our baby boy arrived weeks early and did not survive. Our first pregnancy ended in a miscarriage.

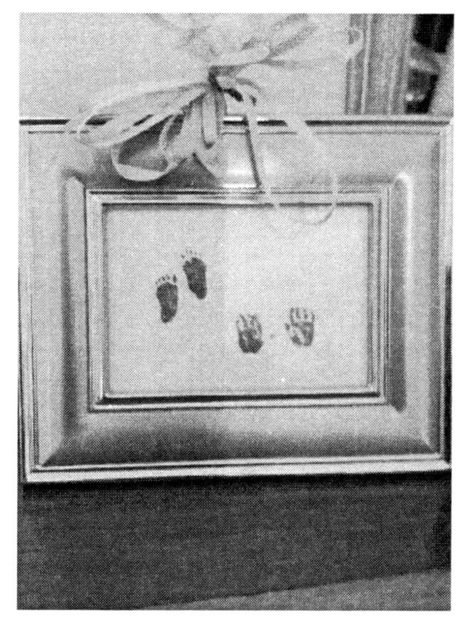

It's part of our story and won't be forgotten. I remember many of the details from that day, the following days and the associated feelings. That's probably why they are so vivid – even years later. We remember how those moments made us feel.

I remember getting the call that my wife had to go to the hospital. I remember the stillbirth and holding my son's body – in one hand. It's an image I can't get out of my head. It's emotional to even write this.

When we went home – just my wife and I, alone – I think I laid in bed for days. We grieved for the child we didn't even know.

Today, every once in a while, I hear of somebody having a rough pregnancy or a miscarriage. I feel terrible for them. Their story brings back my own feelings and emotions. I sometimes cry.

I feel like I can relate, though I don't know what to say to them besides, "I'm sorry."

Losing a child is something nobody should have to go through. But if it happens, we can continue to write our story going forward.

Today, my daughters are healthy and fun – for the most part. I love them and have high hopes for them. That doesn't mean my son's death isn't part of our story. It is. I'm reminded of that when I hear similar stories. I hope my story might inspire others and give them hope. If not today, maybe tomorrow.

Many have told me how thankful they were that I shared this story. I almost didn't. Eight years after it all happened was the first time I published something. When you are ready to share a story, share it. Positive and not so positive stories are worth sharing.

Sometimes we make stories too difficult

Keeping our audience's interest starts with the beginning. Sometimes we set our audiences up for disinterest in our stories. The way we start them, the way we overthink what we know. By way of example, let's use entrepreneurs.

Every so often I run into entrepreneurs and innovators. Some are inside traditional organizations and are attempting to create a new product or service line within an existing structure. Some are starting their own businesses.

As an authentic storyteller, I'm naturally curious and want to know their stories:

- Why did you start doing what you are doing?
- Is it scary?
- How do you find customers?

A million more questions come to mind. Usually, I just ask two in one:

What are you trying to do and why?

Sometimes – many times, really – I get this answer: "It's hard to explain." And then they hop into a lengthy explanation filled with lots of jargon. Really, it doesn't make any difference. Many listeners tune out when told it's "hard to explain."

Innovators, founders, anyone really, who is creating new products, services or businesses needs to be able to explain their ideas simply, clearly and concisely.

If innovators can't explain their own product, how can they expect anyone to understand it?

I've been there myself. It can be hard to explain that in which we are deeply involved. We are so deep in the weeds that we want to explain every single weed to anyone who is standing nearby even if they're really only interested in the big-picture view.

You might wonder: Is he talking about an elevator pitch? Kind of, but don't think of it as pitching. Not everyone is going to want to bat. Just tell them your story. Simply.

Stories come down to:

- What are you trying to do and why?
- What are the barriers and which ones have you overcome already?

Some questions to consider as you are thinking about your response the next time somebody asks about your innovation:

- What do they already know? If they know nothing and you just met them, chances are they are not going to learn everything in the next 10 seconds.
- At the simplest level, what is the innovation for?
- How is it different from existing products?
- What problem is it solving? Being able to say, "I'm working on an app that allows you to avoid long lines at the grocery store" can quickly get the attention of someone who is facing that problem.
- To what is your product similar? Comparing it to something – or maybe a combination of things – that people already are familiar with can paint an immediate picture.

The way you tell your story can build or destroy a business or career. No pressure.

Great stories paint a picture with words

Let's talk some more about what makes great stories. Usually, they have conflict – even if it's minimal – and are authentic. Characters in them are relatable. The stories make us feel something and we can visualize what's happening. It's easier said than done to share our true authentic stories. Many default to telling how great something is versus showing how great it is. Great storytellers show. They don't tell.

One way to share useful stories is to paint a picture with words. We all want to write that attention-grabbing intro and see our content spread – have it be so engaging, people cannot help but share it.

When it works, it works. We know. The audience knows. "Hey, take a look at this!"

When we paint a picture with words, we make an emotional connection with our readers, who then feel more connected to the story they just read. A Los Angeles Times article about a female police forensic unit employee is a good example of this. Here's an excerpt:

> *Gabrielle Wimer was nine months pregnant and working a crime scene when she found the closest thing to a smoking gun for a forensic specialist: a clean, detailed fingerprint.*
>
> *"I was like, 'Oh, I got a beautiful print right here,'" she recalled. "And I turned and my belly just wiped it off." That was it, she said: "I'm done until I have this baby." Now almost 3 years old, Wimer's daughter is still too young to understand her mother's job.*
>
> *All she knows, Wimer said, is that it's for the police. "Police," she'll say. "Mama's work."*

You can probably visualize the scene. I know, I did. Writing like this is powerful and engaging.

I don't remember seeing a picture of Ms. Wimer, but I had a picture in my mind just by reading the intro. When I got to the crime scene part, I pictured her in a crime scene uniform, on the verge of cracking a case. I was rooting for her, even though the story quickly turned with her belly wiping away the print.

I stopped reading, turned to my wife, who was pregnant, and read that part out loud to her. We discussed the story.

Interesting stories have to be shared

Breaking it down: Paint a picture with words

When we paint a picture with words, we help stories separate themselves from all the noise out there. Stories like this stand out and are:

- Memorable
- Easily retold
- Emotional (I totally felt bad for the officer)
- Interesting

We might not care about an overarching, statistical kind of story. But we care about people and emotions.

The trick is finding the right words to paint the picture. Sharing detailed stories about something that's not interesting or relevant won't draw anyone in. Picking the right words to paint the right picture helps us tell better, more engaging stories.

It's probably not as complicated as we think it is. In addition to showing and not telling, we also want to make sure to simplify! Just not to the level of inaccuracy. Let's not let great stories die because we think they are so hard to share. Some days, it seems that the first step to authentic storytelling actually is: Stop overthinking everything.

"This can't be explained in 10 seconds." "No elevator ride is long enough to give this story justice." You've probably heard these excuses before. Another favorite of mine is, "Words can't describe it."

If words can't, what can?

Sometimes we get seduced into believing that complexity is good. We mastered and understood a complex item, so we need to keep it complex to not diminish its intellectual value.

But as Albert Einstein once said: "You don't understand it well enough if you can't explain it simply."

Explaining things simply helps people understand. And it actually establishes the storyteller as an expert: "Wow! That made sense. She explained that so well. I get it."

And how do we know people get it? They can actually retell the content.

Perhaps this has happened in your household: A person goes to the doctor. The doctor explains the problem in detail, with lots of industry-specific jargon. The person forgets most of that lingo the second they hear it. At home, the person's spouse asks about the details. All the person shares is, "I have to have surgery. There's something wrong with my stomach."

Some complex details just can't be re-shared by non-expert listeners, so we have to make it simpler. Or maybe it's that we *get* to explain it simply. Not everyone can do this, so helping people understand can build relationships.

There's no reason to hide behind complexity – unless we have something to hide, which, of course, would be an entirely different discussion about authenticity and transparency. Sharing information in a simple way helps us be and appear authentic and transparent. And, yes, a lot of times simple means that content is fairly short and memorable.

But using plain English to share your stories can be harder than it sounds. Many industries and groups use jargon and acronyms that don't make much sense to the general public. Stories that are published (especially on our websites) should make sense to that sixth-grade level reader.

As organizations continue to move toward telling authentic stories and away from the more traditional messaging approach, communicator roles will evolve into trainers and translators for subject matter experts.

Many organizations (past and present) have spokespeople who do the public speaking/messaging for an organization. But they aren't the subject-matter experts. They might be really good at talking in soundbites, writing copy that has a mass audience appeal and other related public relations' skills.

But is that the best approach?

I think the definition of who should be an organization's spokesperson could evolve over the next few years. I predict more organizations will have their subject-matter experts become their spokespeople. Communication team members can assist those experts in their communication skills and also in translating jargon into plain English, if need be.

Some history

In many organizations, marketing and communications staffers gather the information that needs to be disseminated. Sometimes that's done based on a reporter's questions following an interview request.

The communications person then finds the subject-matter expert, asks the questions and takes the answers back to the reporter, who usually has follow-up questions. The public relations person might not have the answers but checks with the expert again.

As you may imagine, this can go on for a while. And it's probably not a very enjoyable situation for any of the parties involved. The reporter is probably pushing a deadline, and the interview is taking longer than it should. The public relations person is getting tired of running back and forth, interrupting the expert. And the expert probably isn't finding this the most productive use of time either.

Why do we even have spokespeople?

Probably because it's easier to control the message when only one person is speaking publicly. I do think there's still a place for this approach – in a big emergency, for example. But that's the exception.

Today

It's hard to control any kind of message today anyway. People say whatever they want on social media. They may blog about a topic that touches a business' interests. And people may even read these things! Sometimes it's shared. Every once in a while, a story goes "viral." Even if a story doesn't go viral, it might still reach the right people who are impacted by it and can impact you and your relationships.

So it's important that everyone, to a degree, sees themselves as a spokesperson for their employer – especially about their area of expertise and the basics of an organization.

For example, people ask me all kinds of things about where I work. I should be able to answer many of those questions because I have a basic understanding of the organization, its mission and what it does. Most of those answers should be on an organization's website, too.

How to communicate publicly

The key to public communication is that I can put my answers in my own words. If I can't do that and instead must recite memorized marketing talking points, my message won't be authentic or believable.

Only a person's own words come across as authentic and truthful. Yes, some of us can fake it, but often that works only to a degree, and it isn't sustainable.

Authenticity, believability and clarity are sustainable and build relationships over the long term.

It'll grow fairly slowly, but remember that most over-night successes take a few years. Once you've set your mind to continuously publish and participate authentically, you'll see increases in readership, participation and business relationships.

Spotting stories

Specificity can help you find stories if your organization has started to share its authentic success stories.

Asking these questions will help your organization spot stories:

- What happened today that stood out to me?
- What surprised me today?
- What will I share with a friend or significant other tonight?
- Of all the things that happened today, which one made the biggest impact on my organization?
- What was on my team's agenda today?
- What's the most important and urgent project right now?

Some of the answers to these questions probably couldn't be published; the answers might include confidential information. And that's OK – you don't have to share those pieces.

But they're starting points to help you come up with stories that your organization might consider sharing publicly through its website and social channels and even pitch to relevant media companies for further coverage. They go deeper than the traditional marketing dribble.

I hope you will embark on this journey to share your authentic story with me. When we all share our unique experiences and knowledge, we can learn from each other and can help each other be as successful as possible. All of us. There's an abundance of great stories. Unfortunately, there's also an abundance of stories that go untold. Don't let your great stories die.

Acknowledgments

I would like to thank my fantabulous wife, Rachel, who puts up with my storytelling talk and always sends a smile my way, usually over FaceTime when I'm flying around the globe to encourage people to share their own authentic stories.

My daughters who certainly are growing up to not live with the status quo. They are kind of stubborn, like me. It can get old from time to time. Ha.

Thanks to MedTouch Managing Partner Sandra Fancher for encouraging me to finally put this book together, and to my content marketing team at MedTouch for being an awesome, supportive group of go-getters with a can-do attitude.

Thanks to Chuck Peters, Chairman of The Gazette Company, a regional media company in Iowa, for his mentorship over the years.

Thanks to my editors Mary Sharp and Mariah Obiedzinski.

Thanks to John Paul Schaffer for the awesome cover design.

Finally, there are many more in the content marketing community who encouraged and influenced my path, way too many to list them all here. Thanks to all of you.

One last thought

I hope this book and my blog at AuthenticStorytelling.net inspire you to share more authentic stories. To do that, we first have to live them. It can lead to a better life for us and those around us. Let's go for it!

Up next

My next two books will focus on content marketing journalism and what it really means to be user-centric. I'm sure I'll announce their release on my blog at AuthenticStorytelling.net.

Ongoing

To book me to speak at your conference or train your team, here's my booking information:

Christoph Trappe
ctrappe@christophtrappe.com
319-804-9853